Alabama

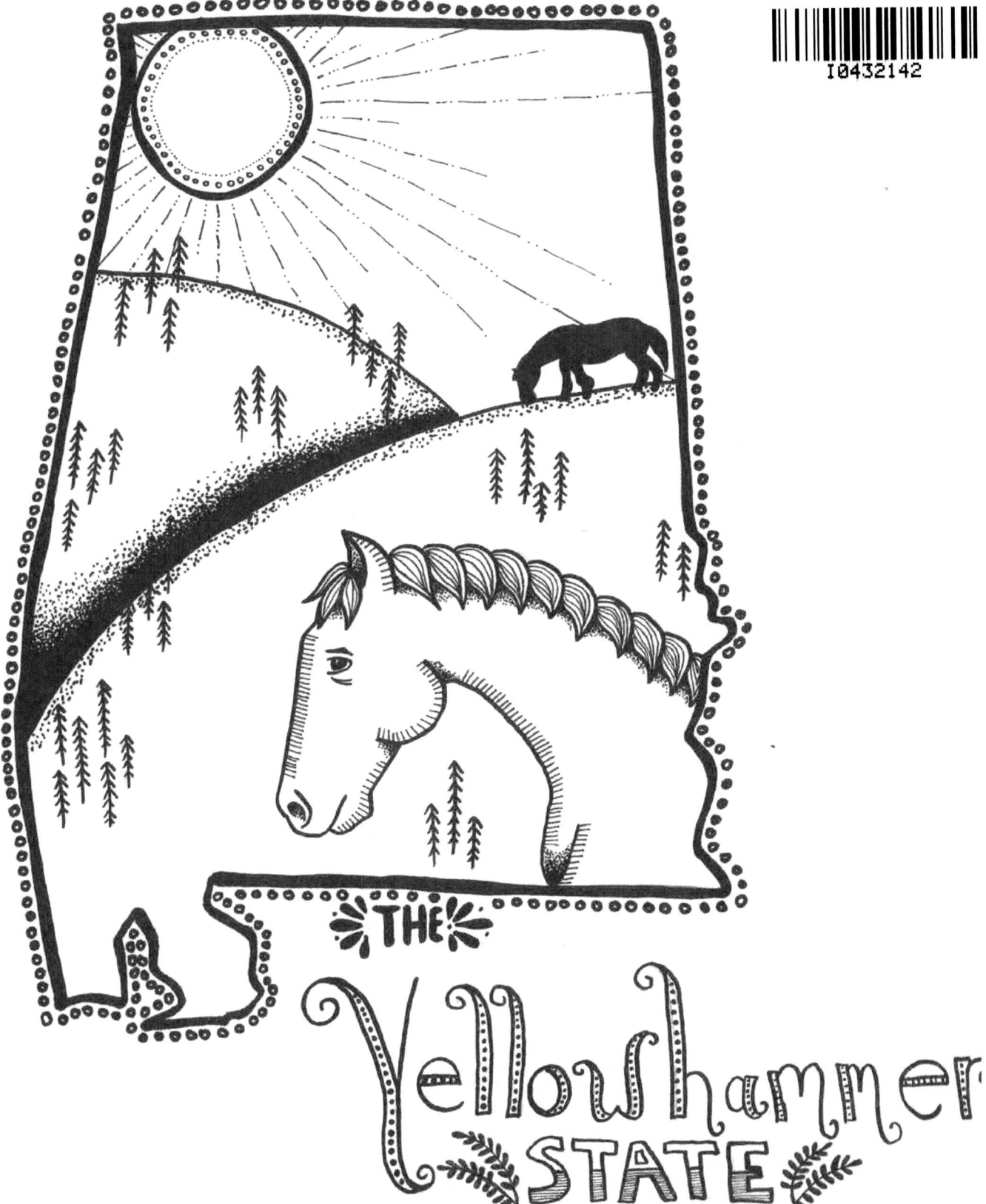

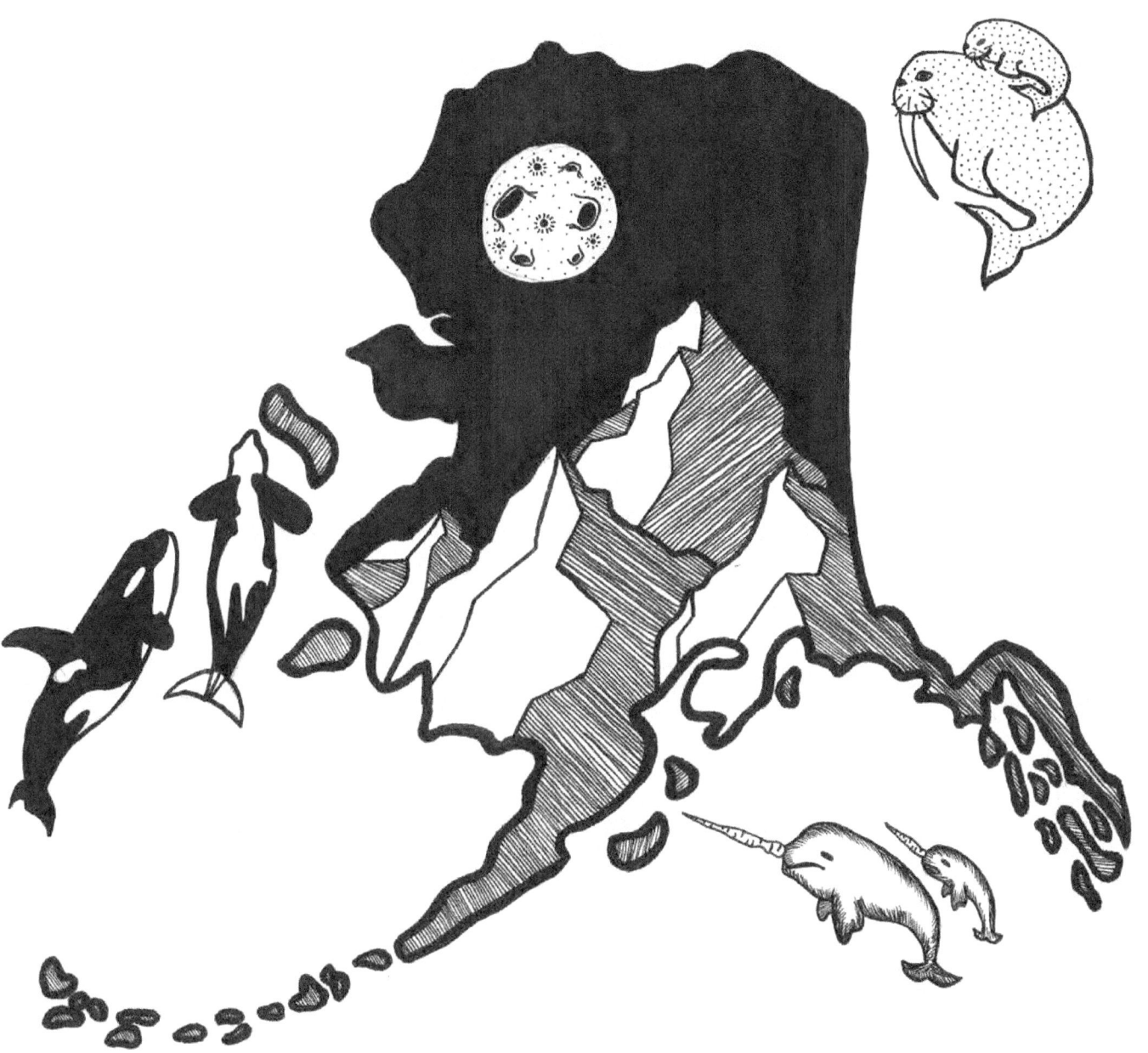

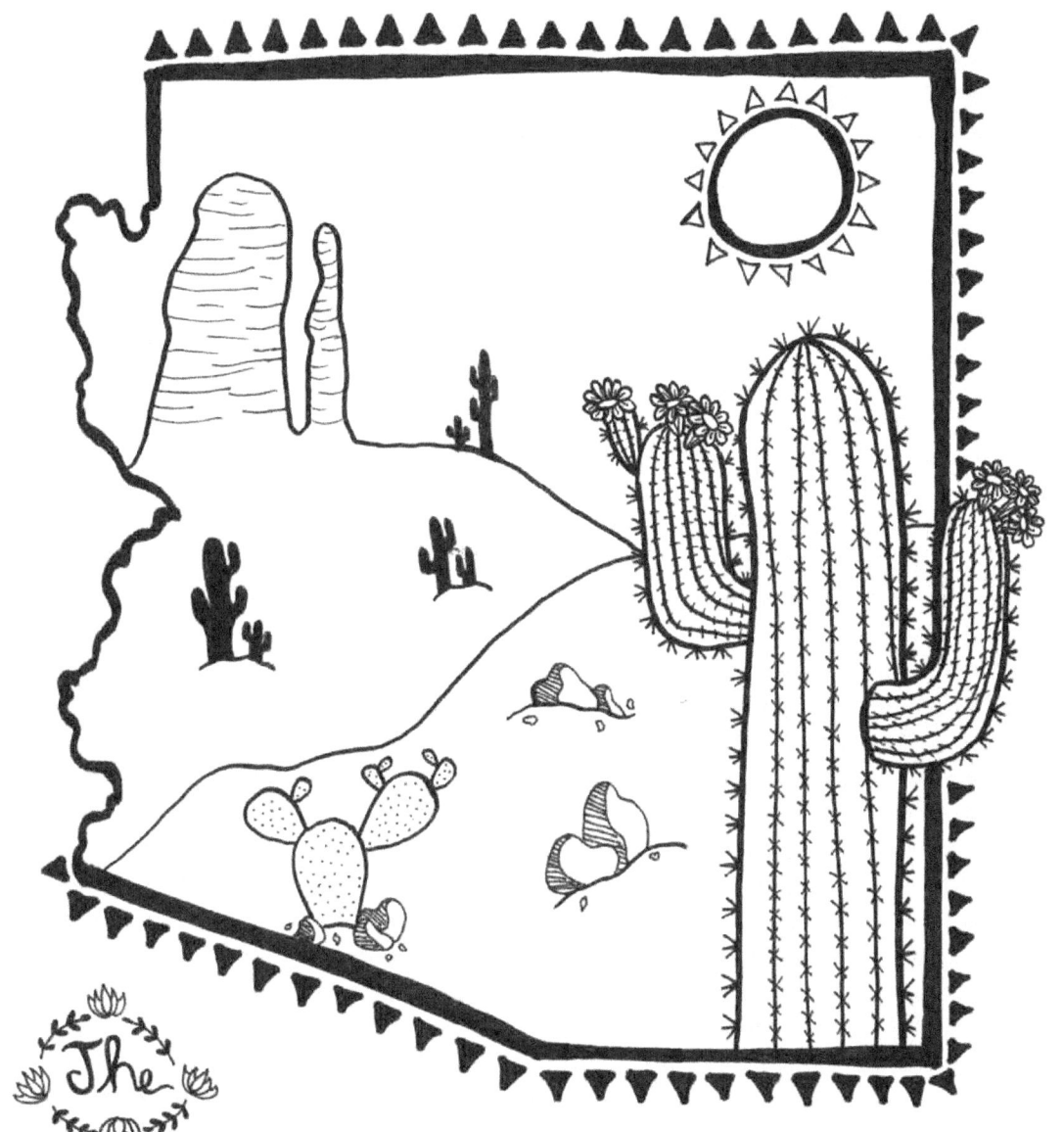

Arkansas

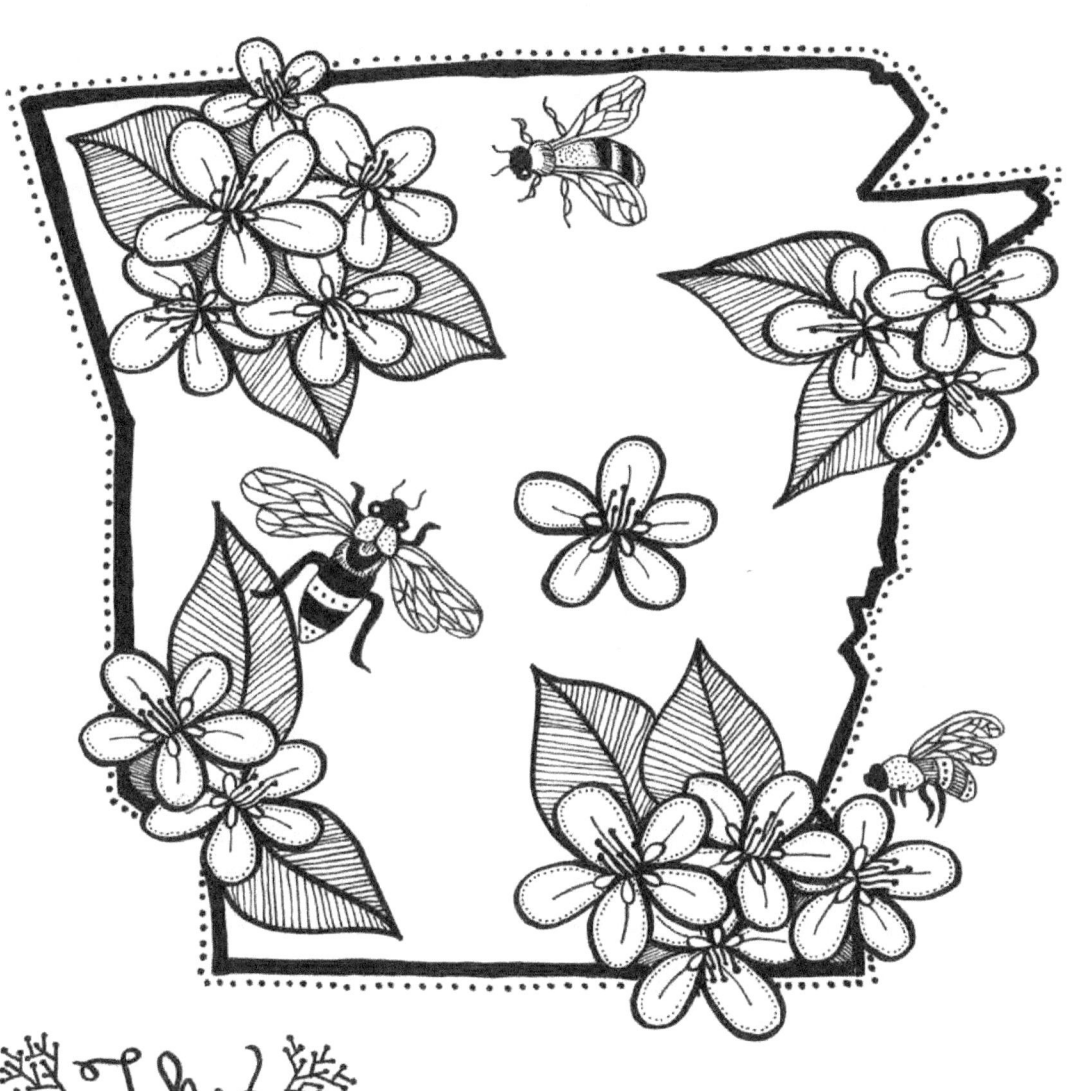

California

THE GOLDEN STATE

Colorado

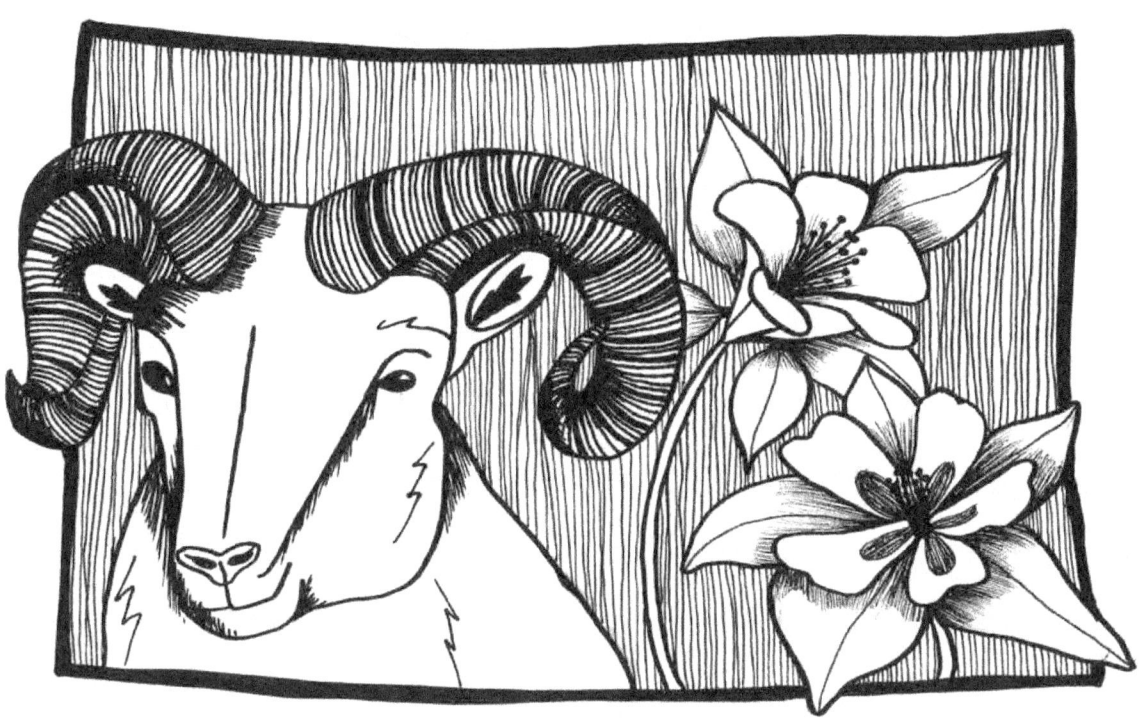

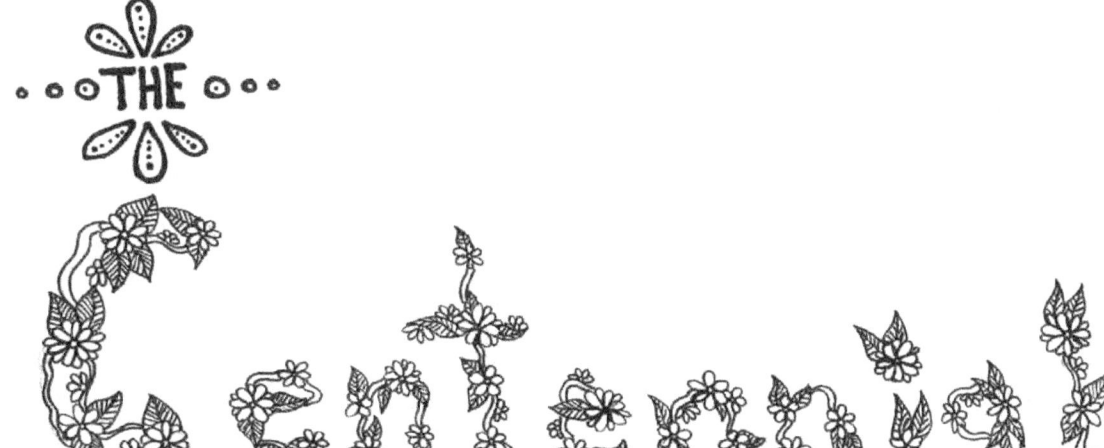

STATE

Connecticut

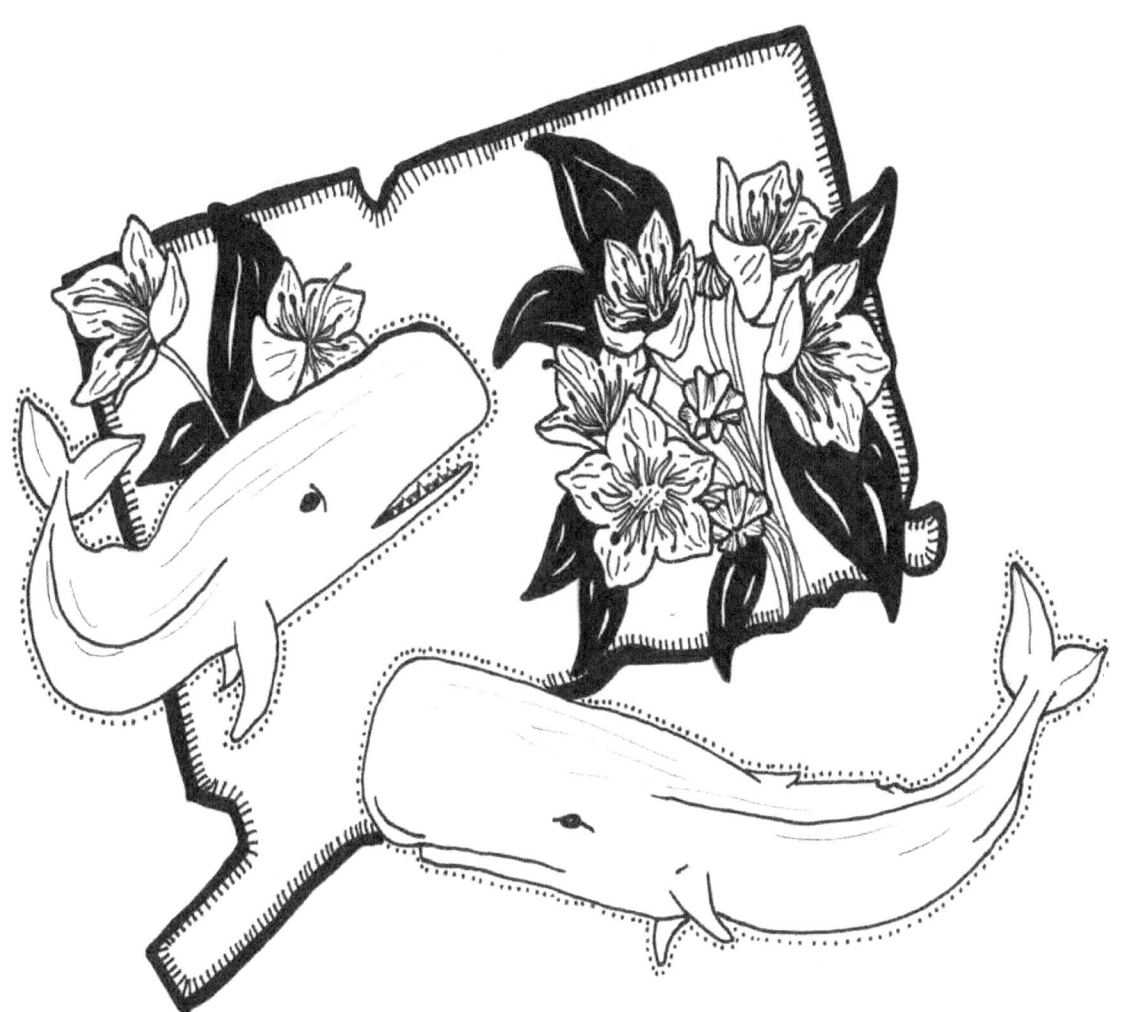

THE CONSTITUTION STATE

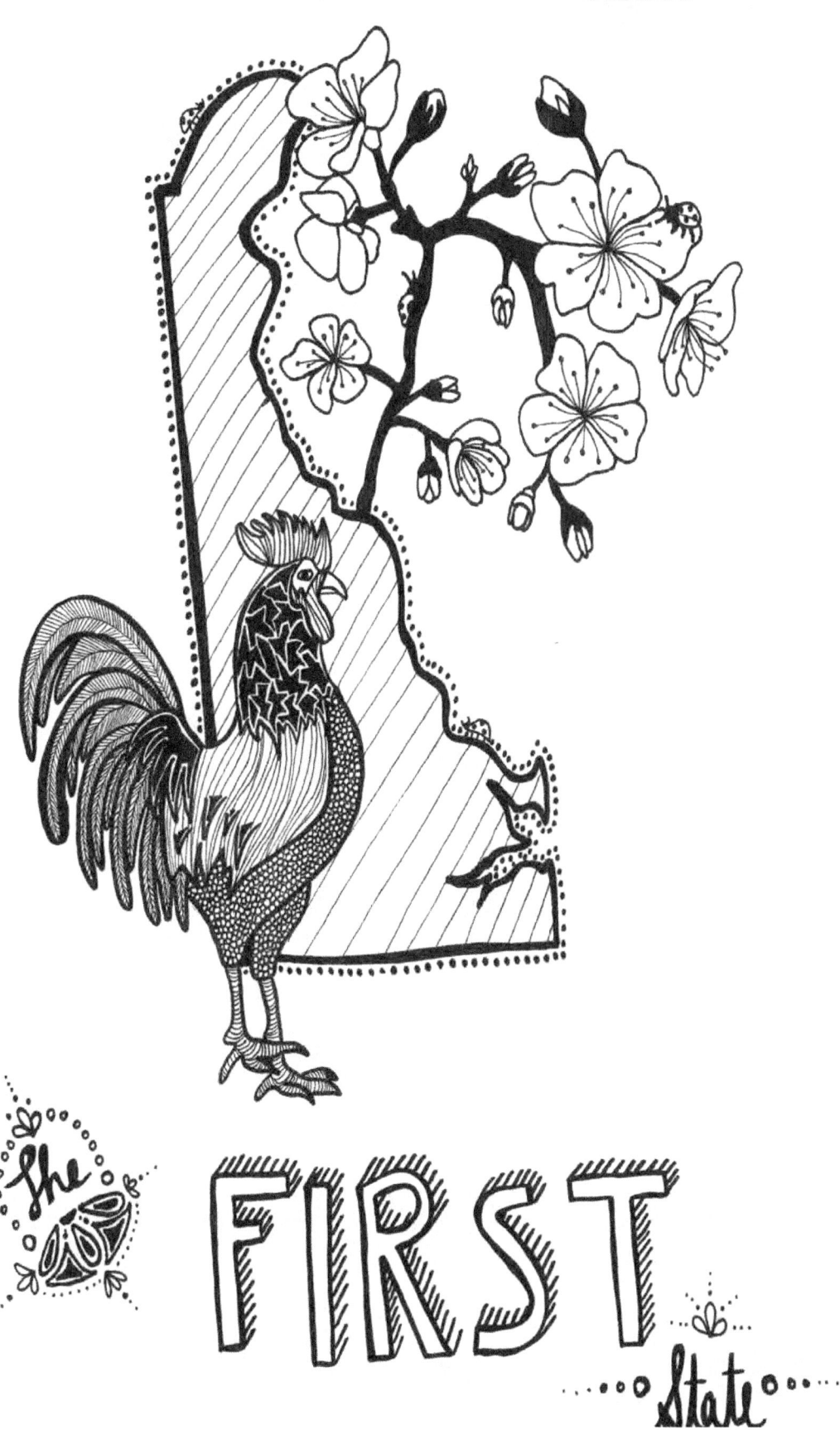

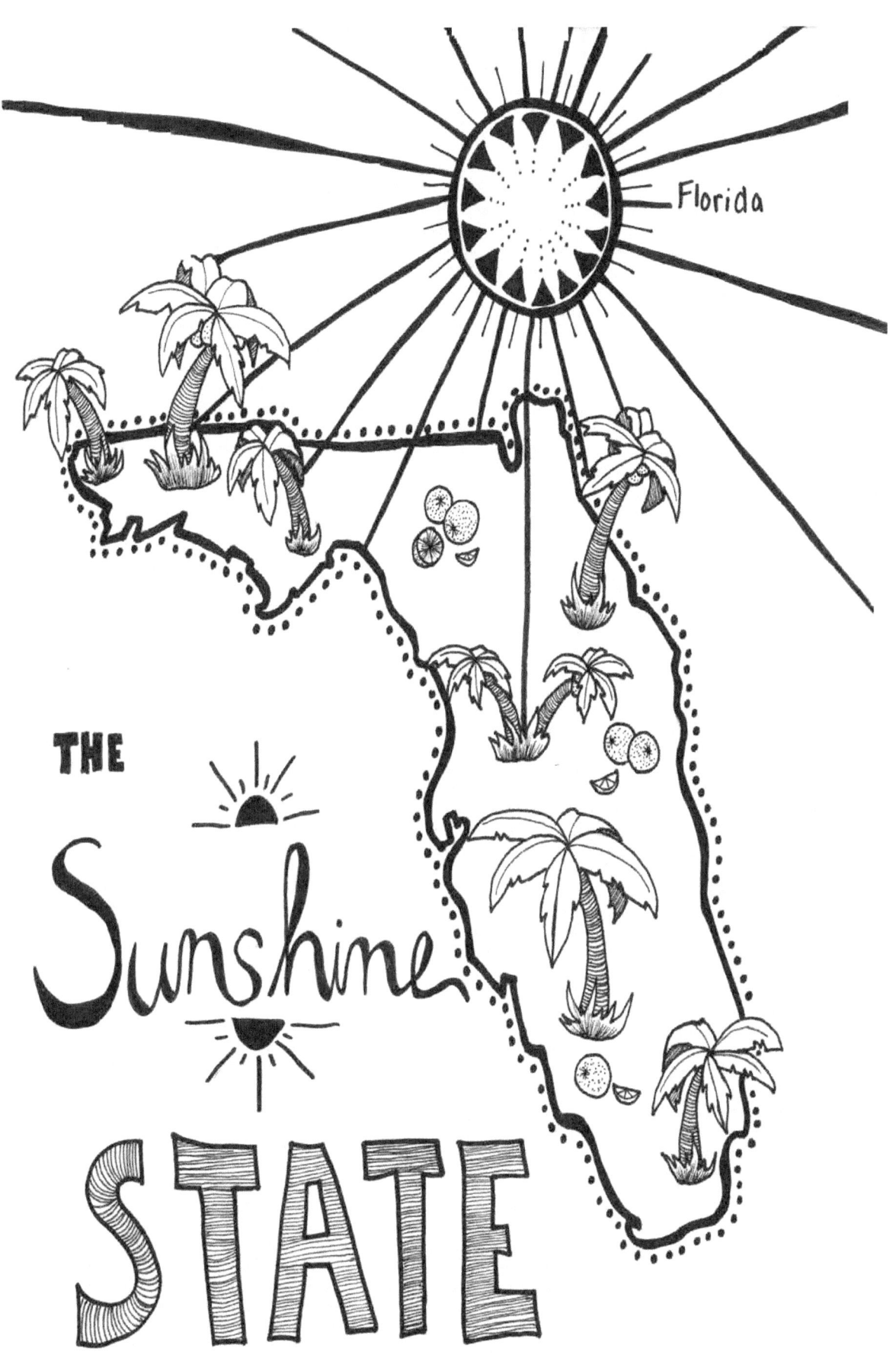

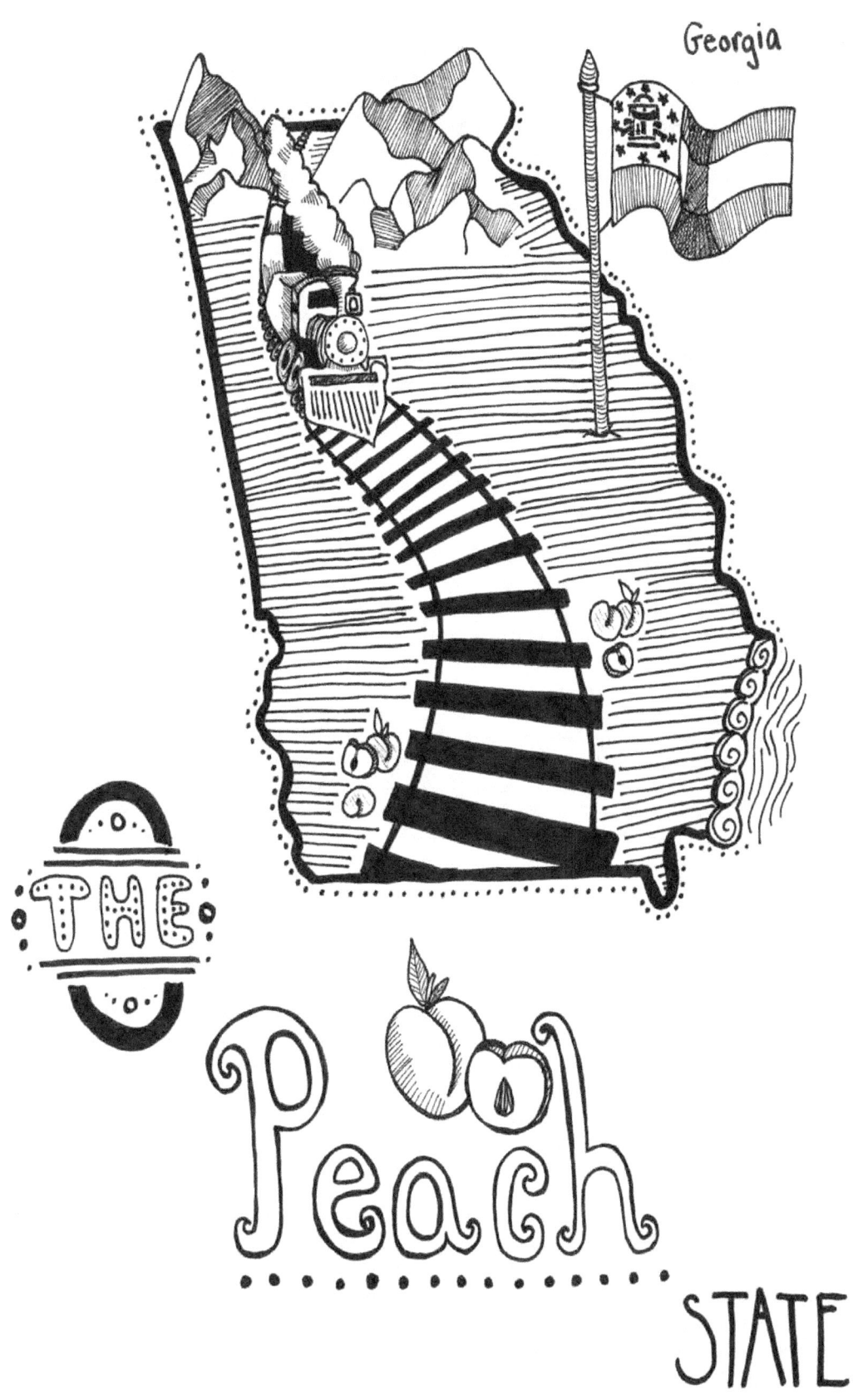

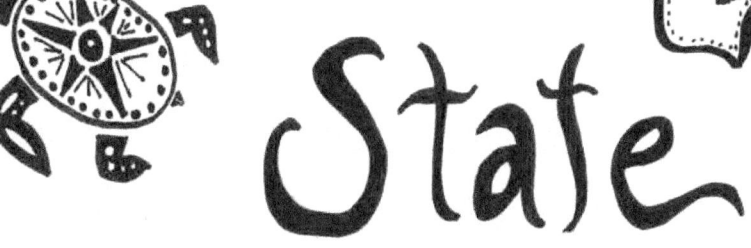

Idaho

THE GEM
STATE

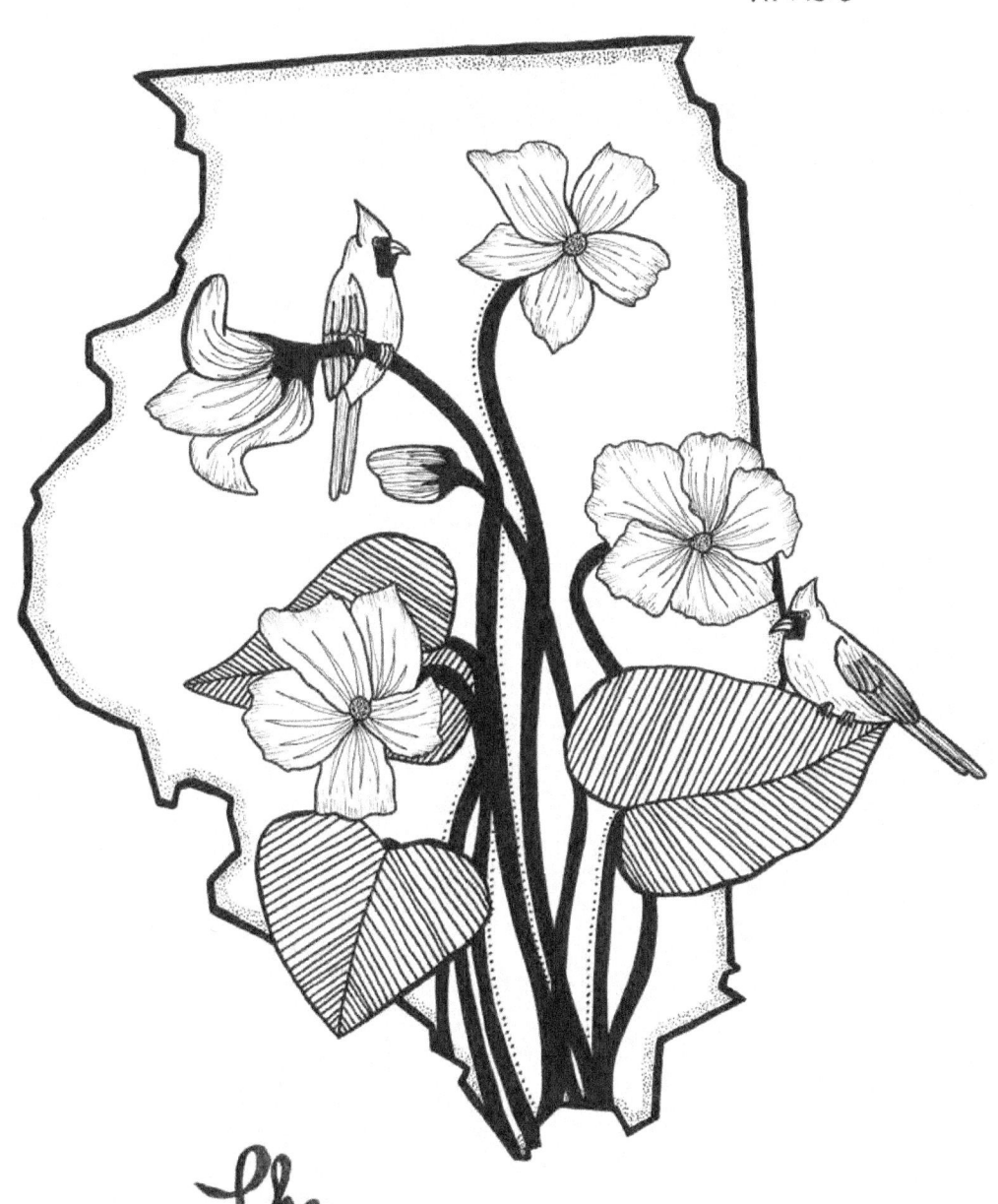

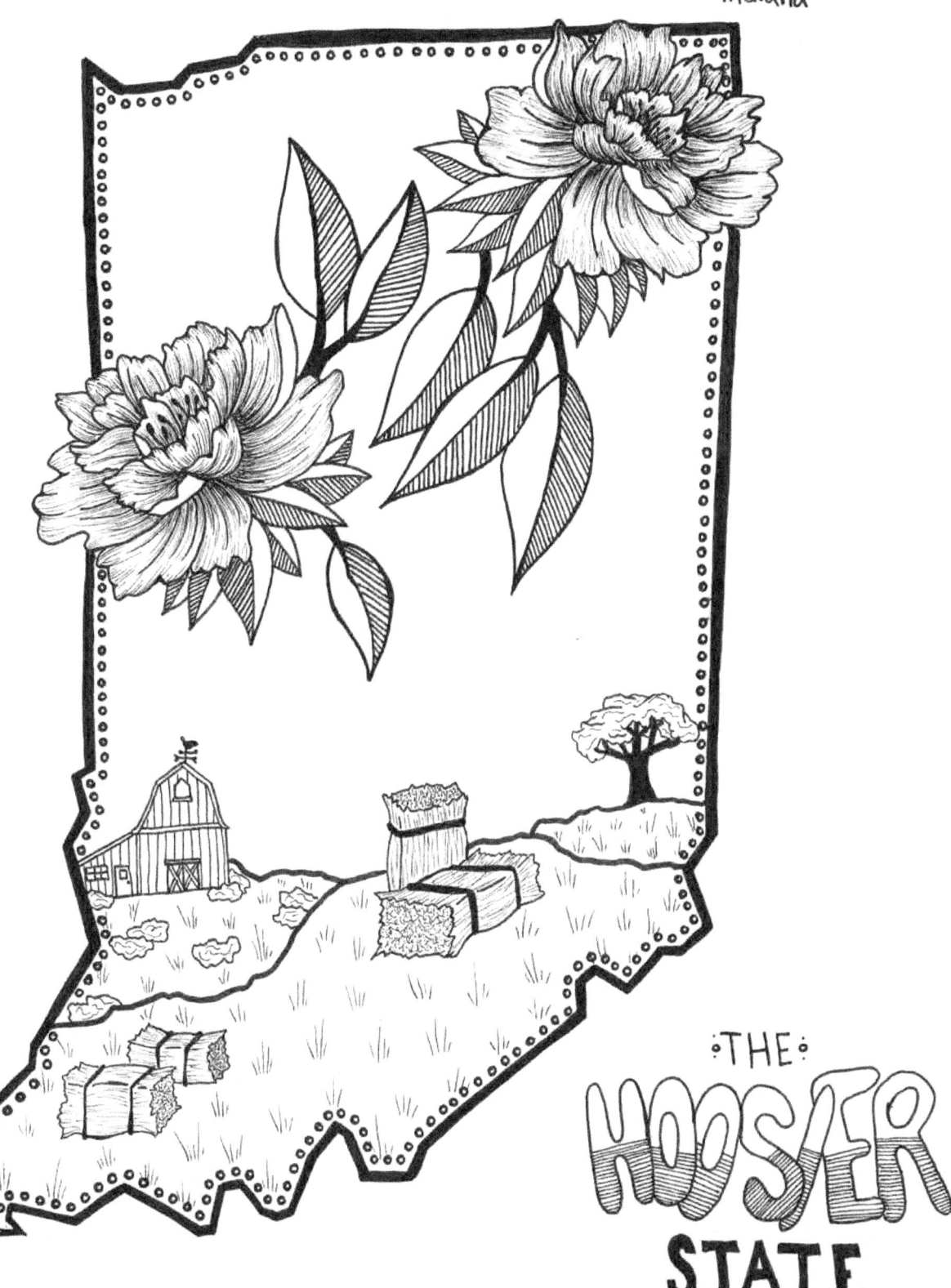

Iowa

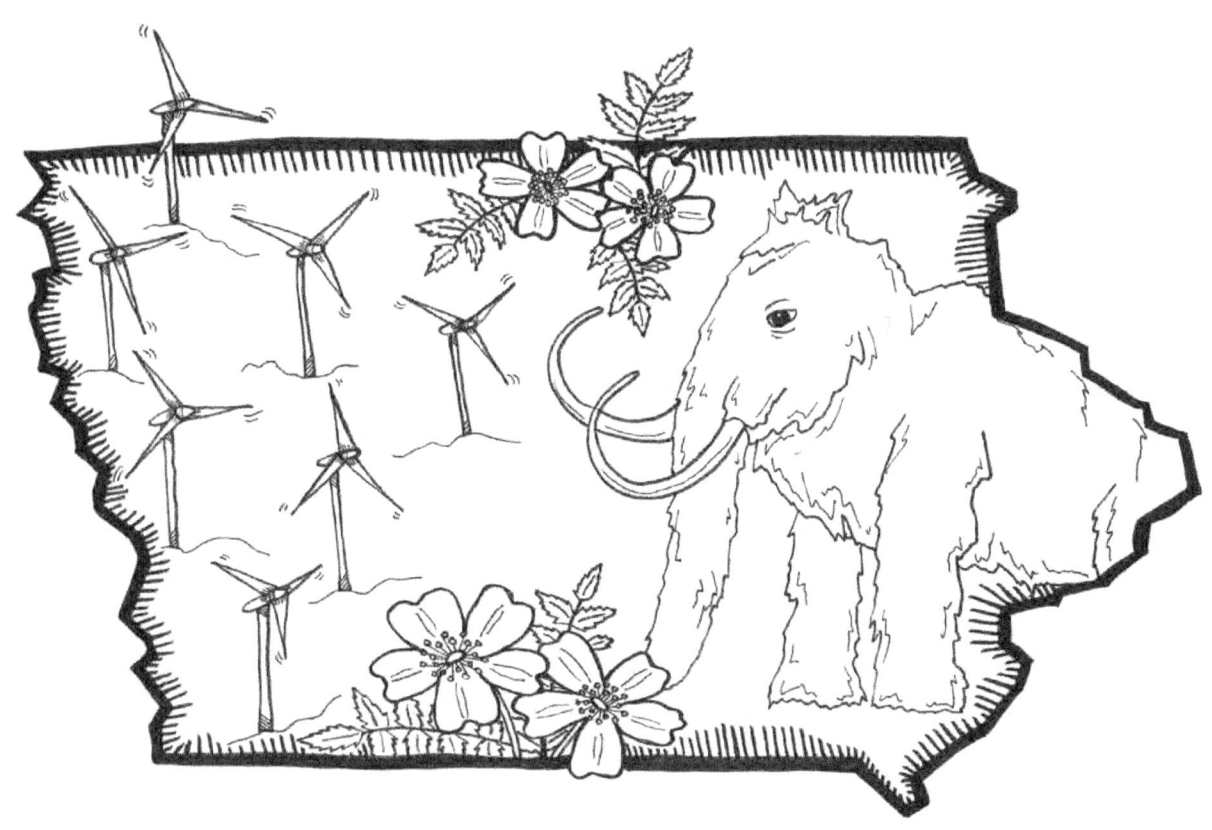

THE
HAWKEYE
STATE

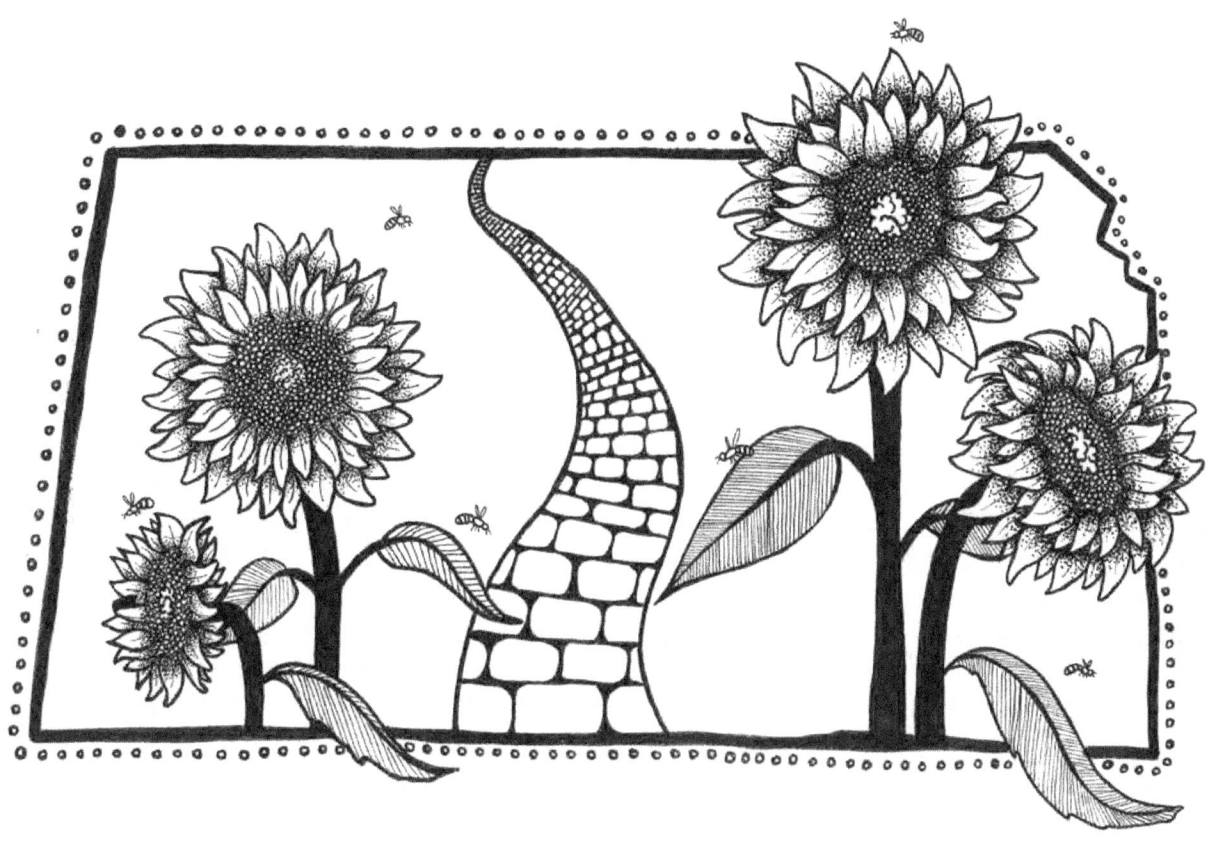

Kentucky

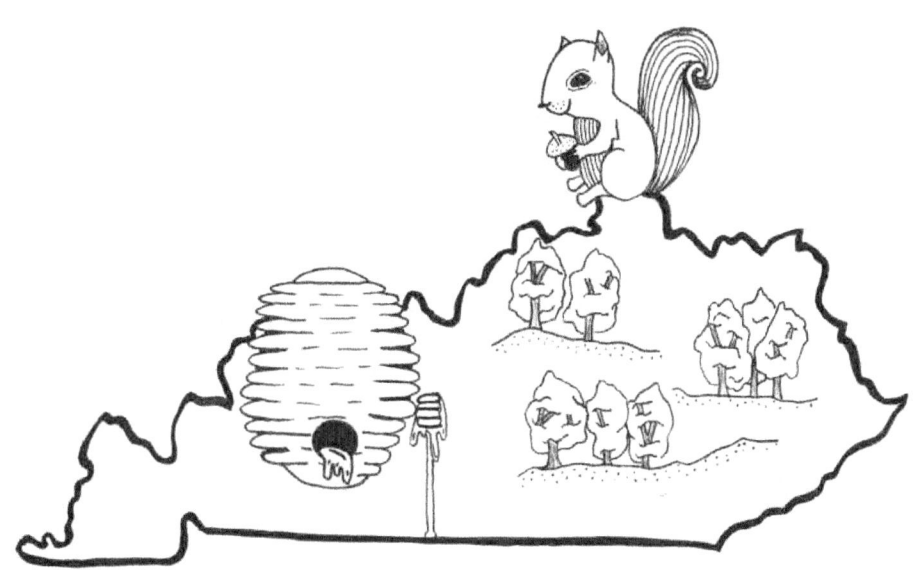

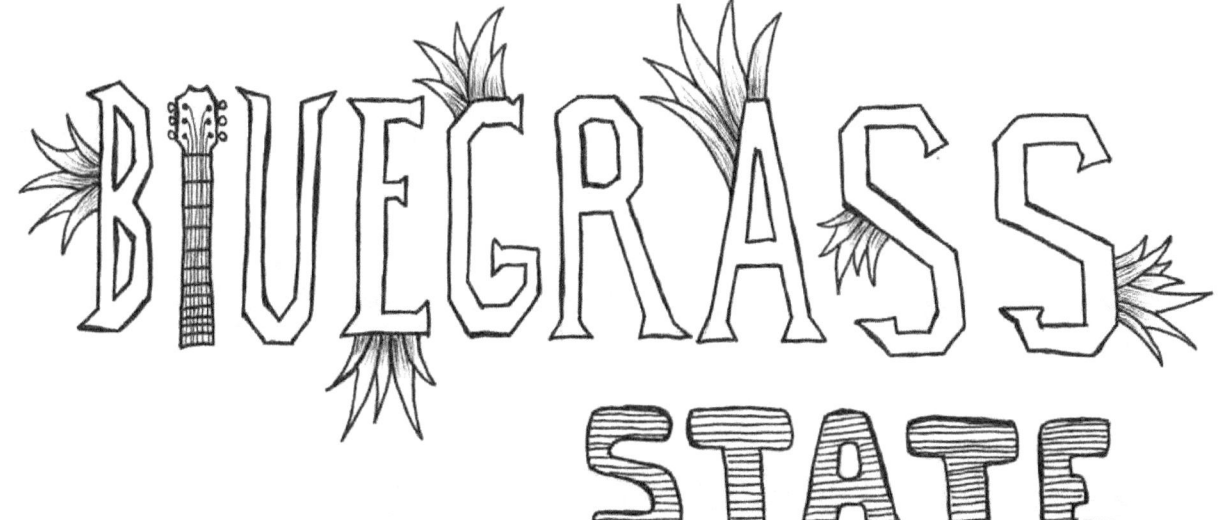

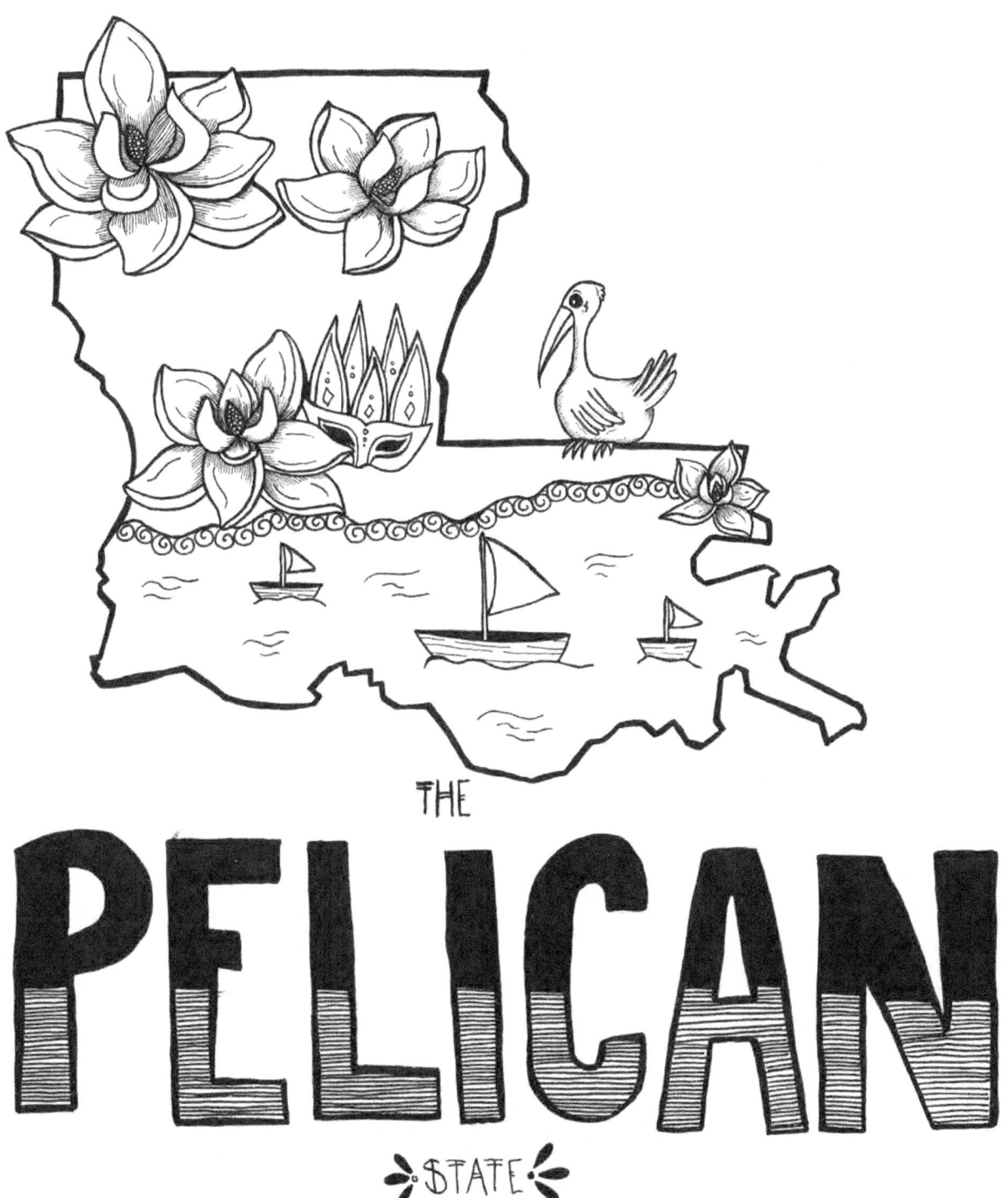

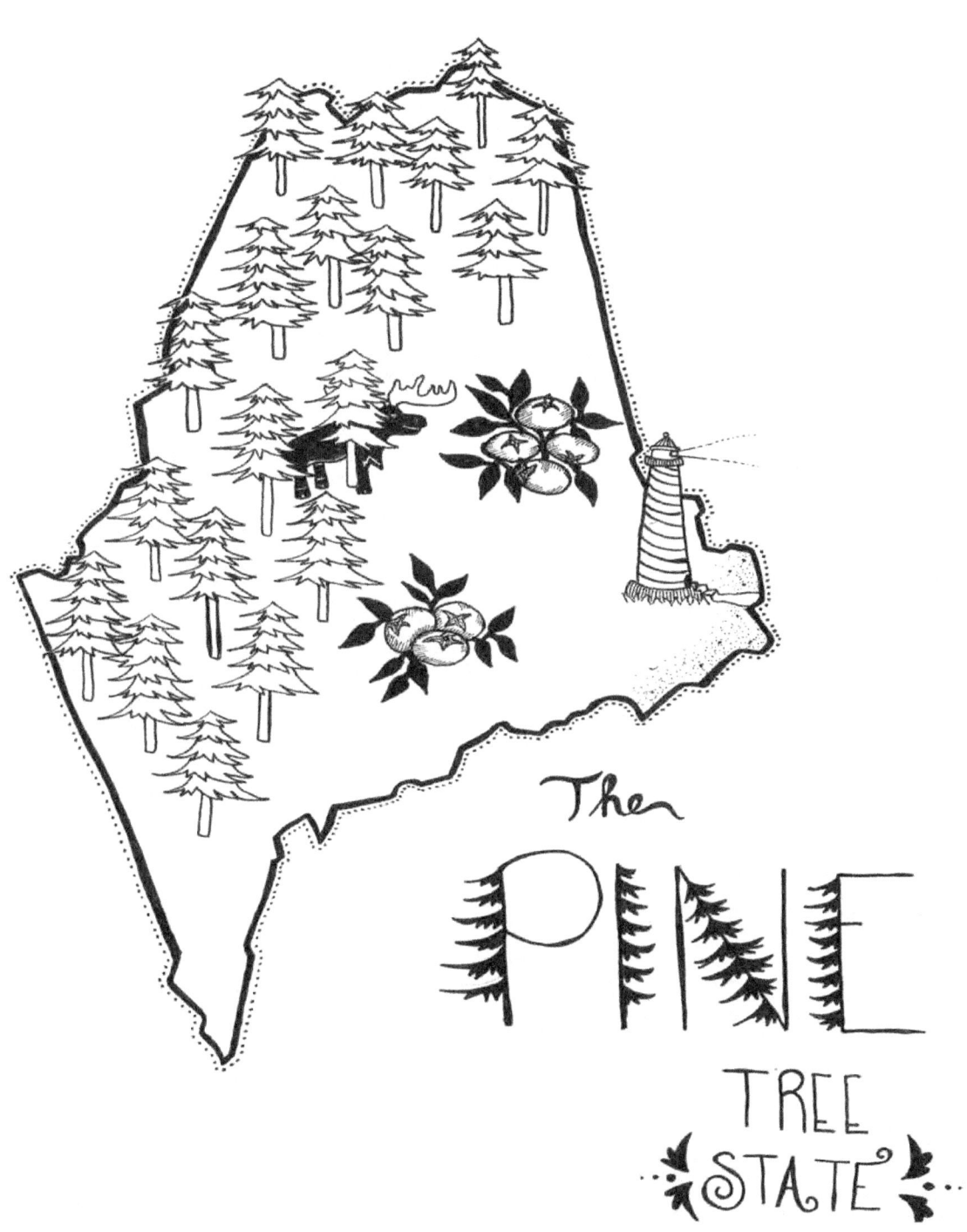

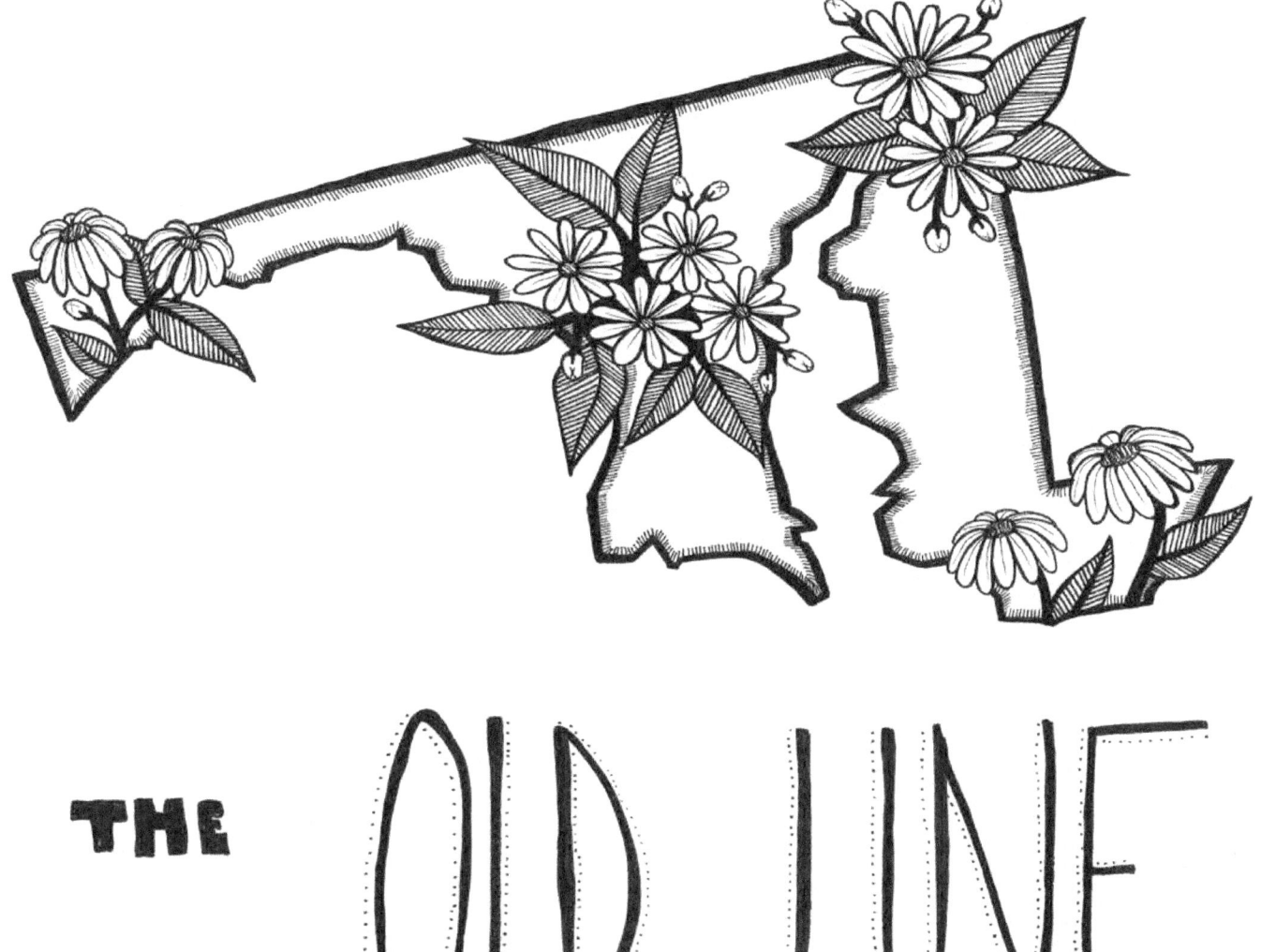

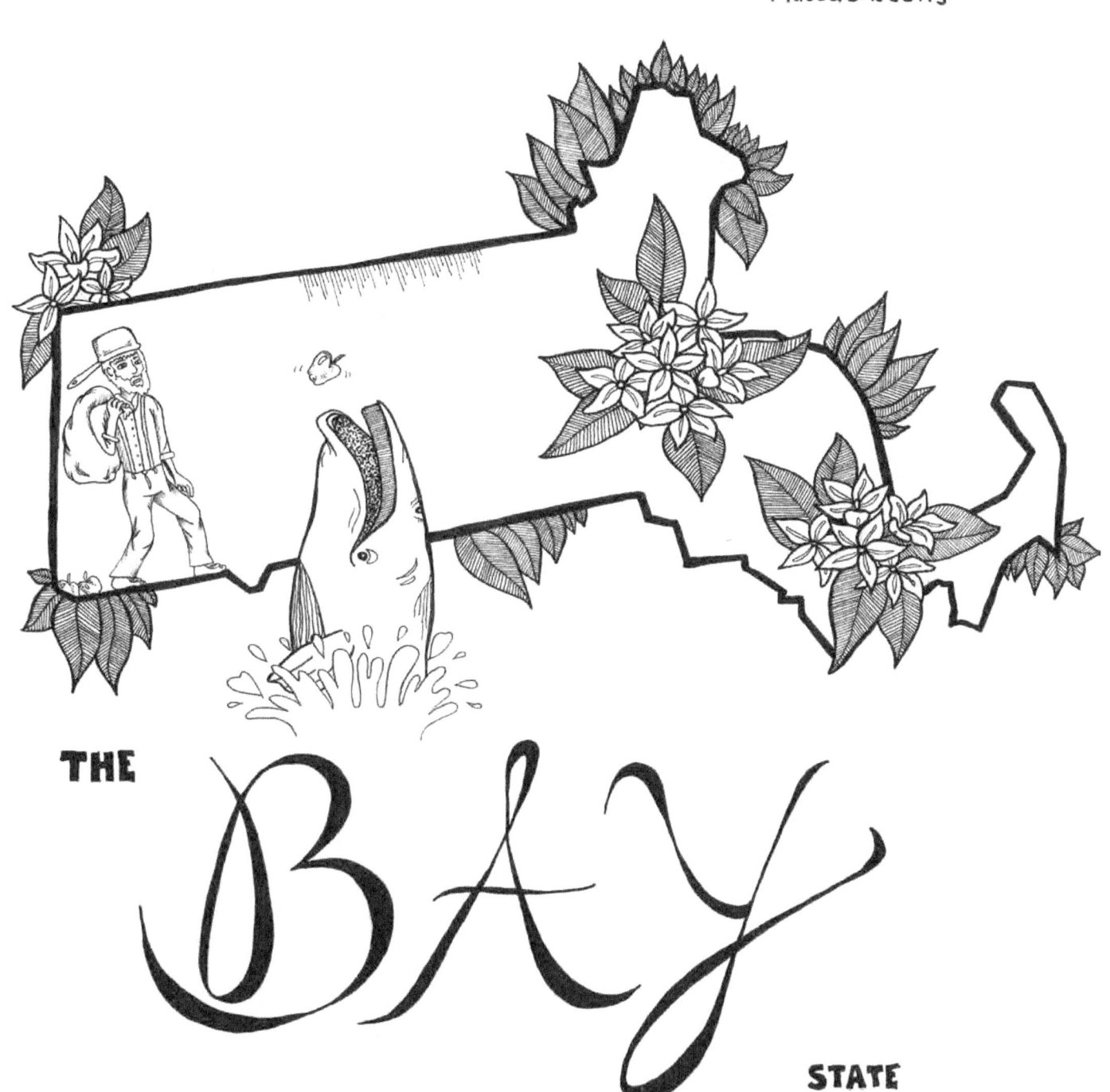

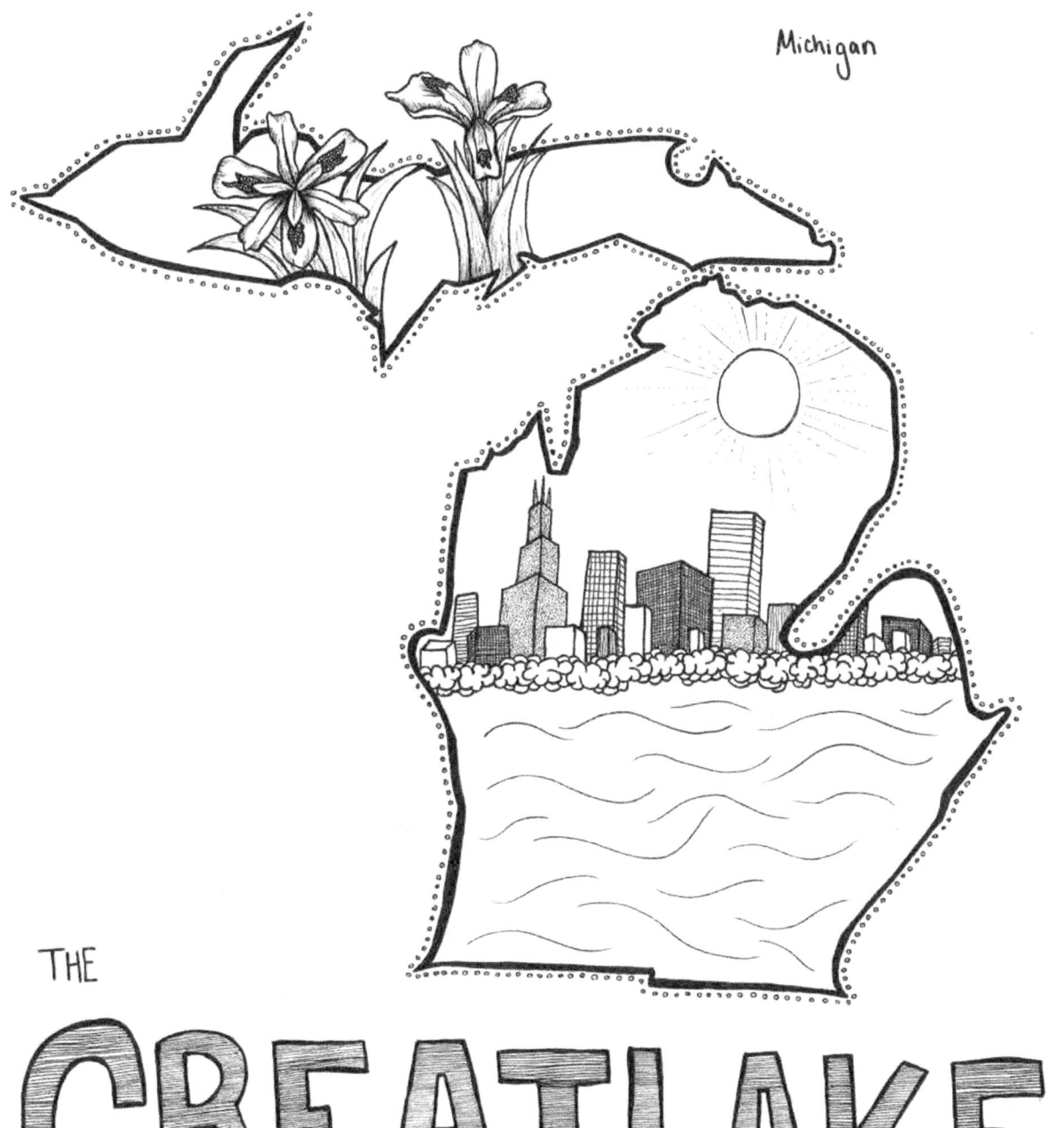

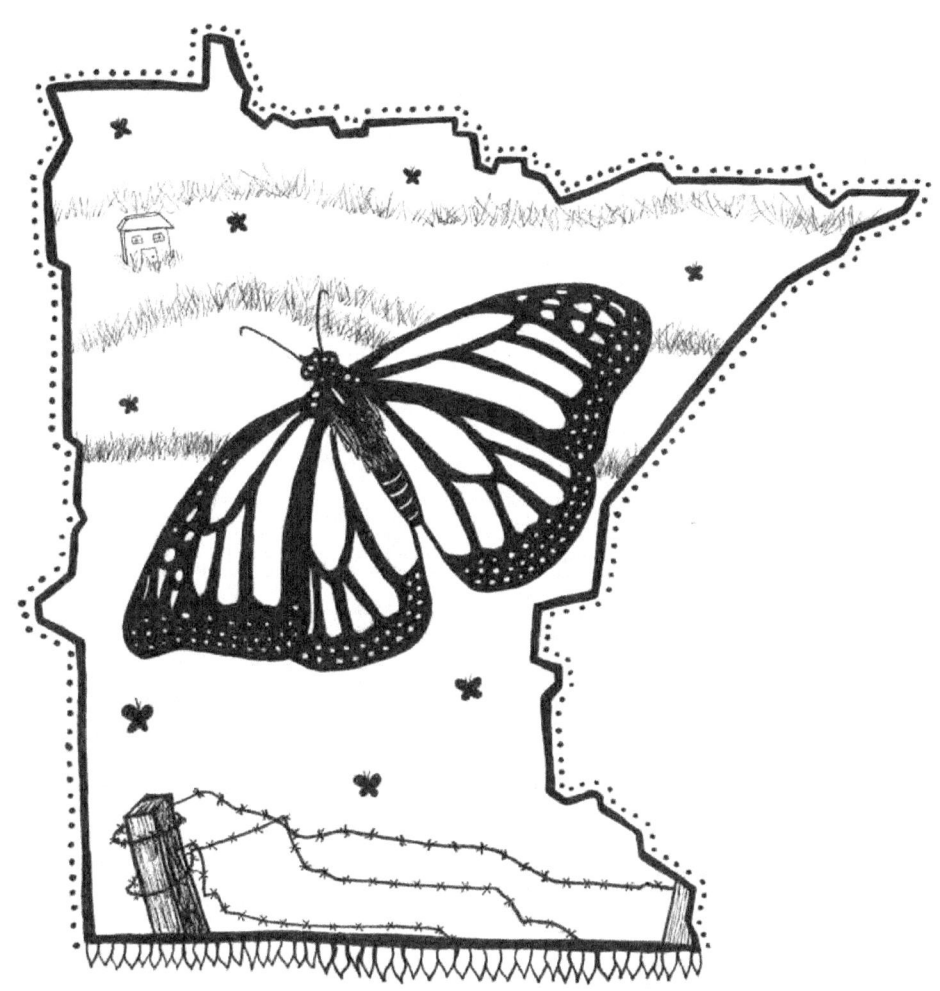

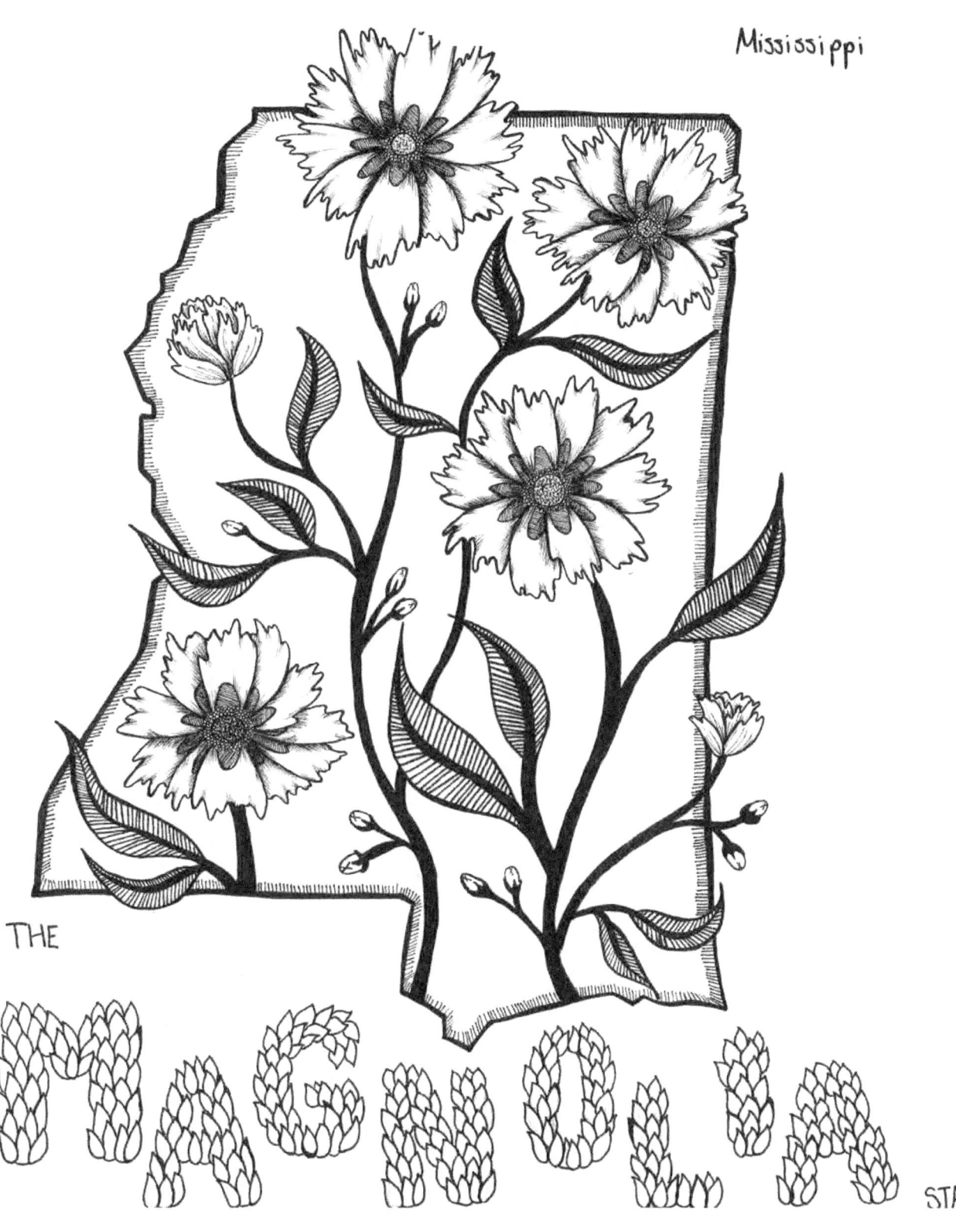

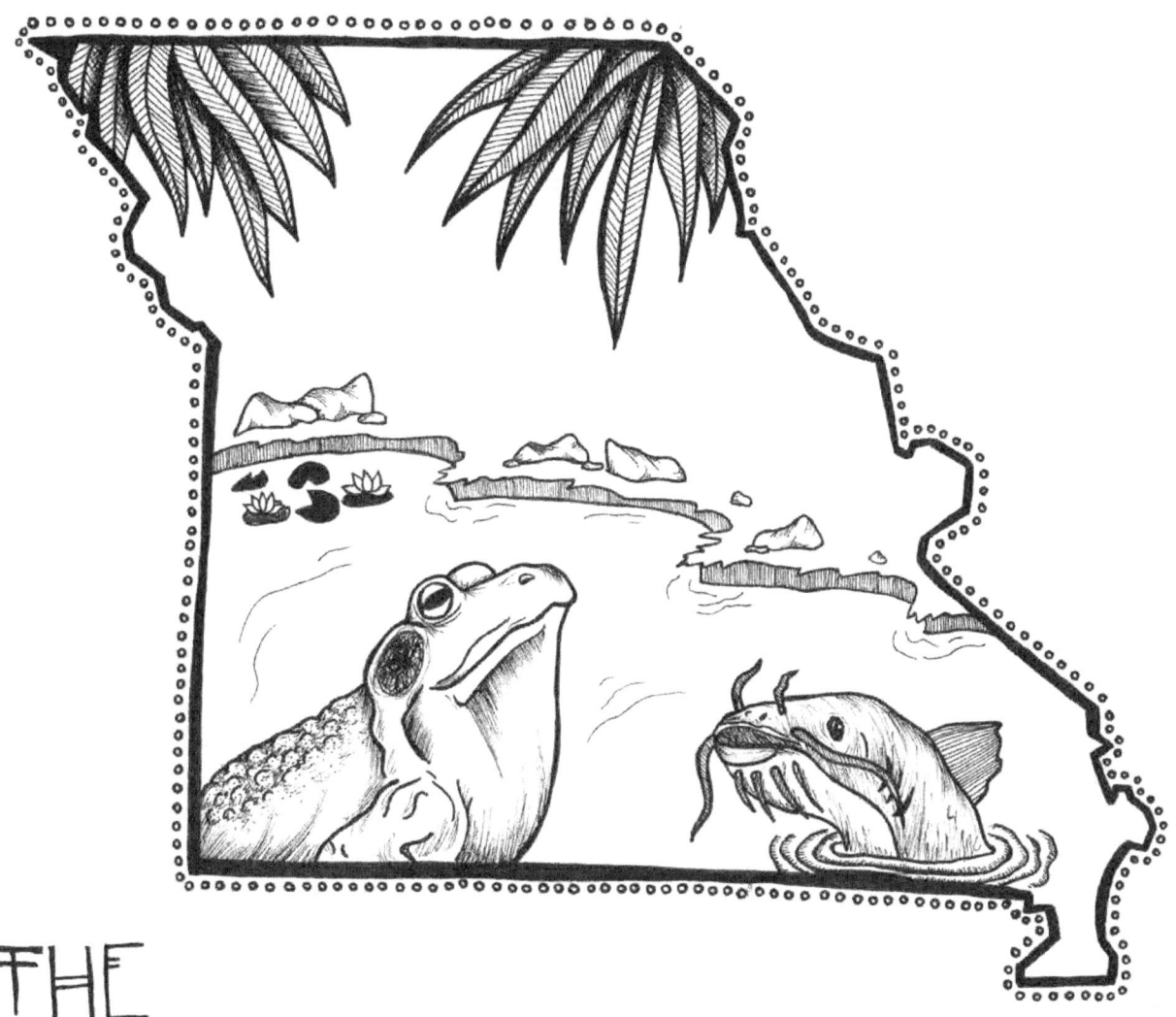

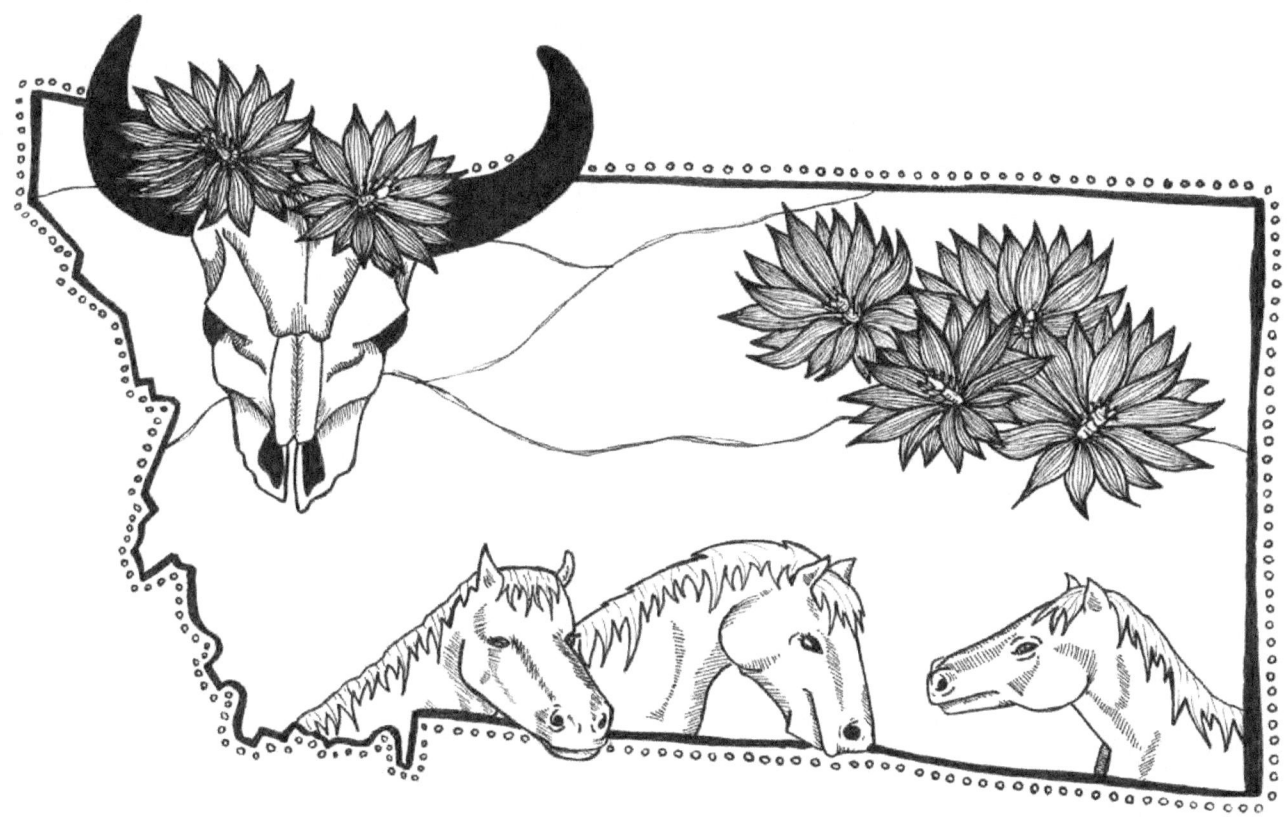

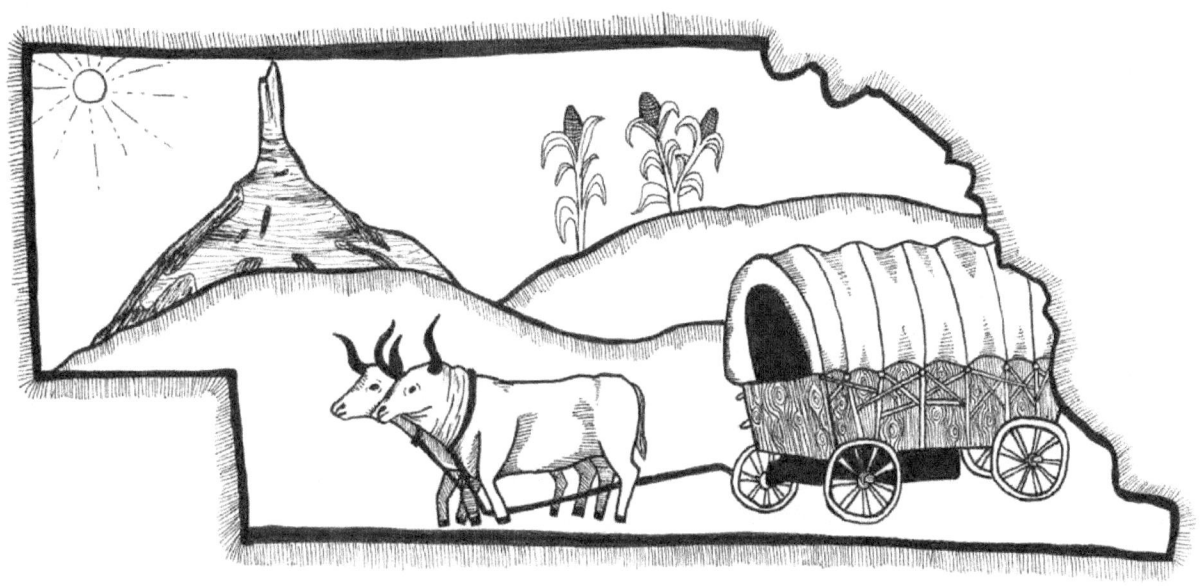

Nevada

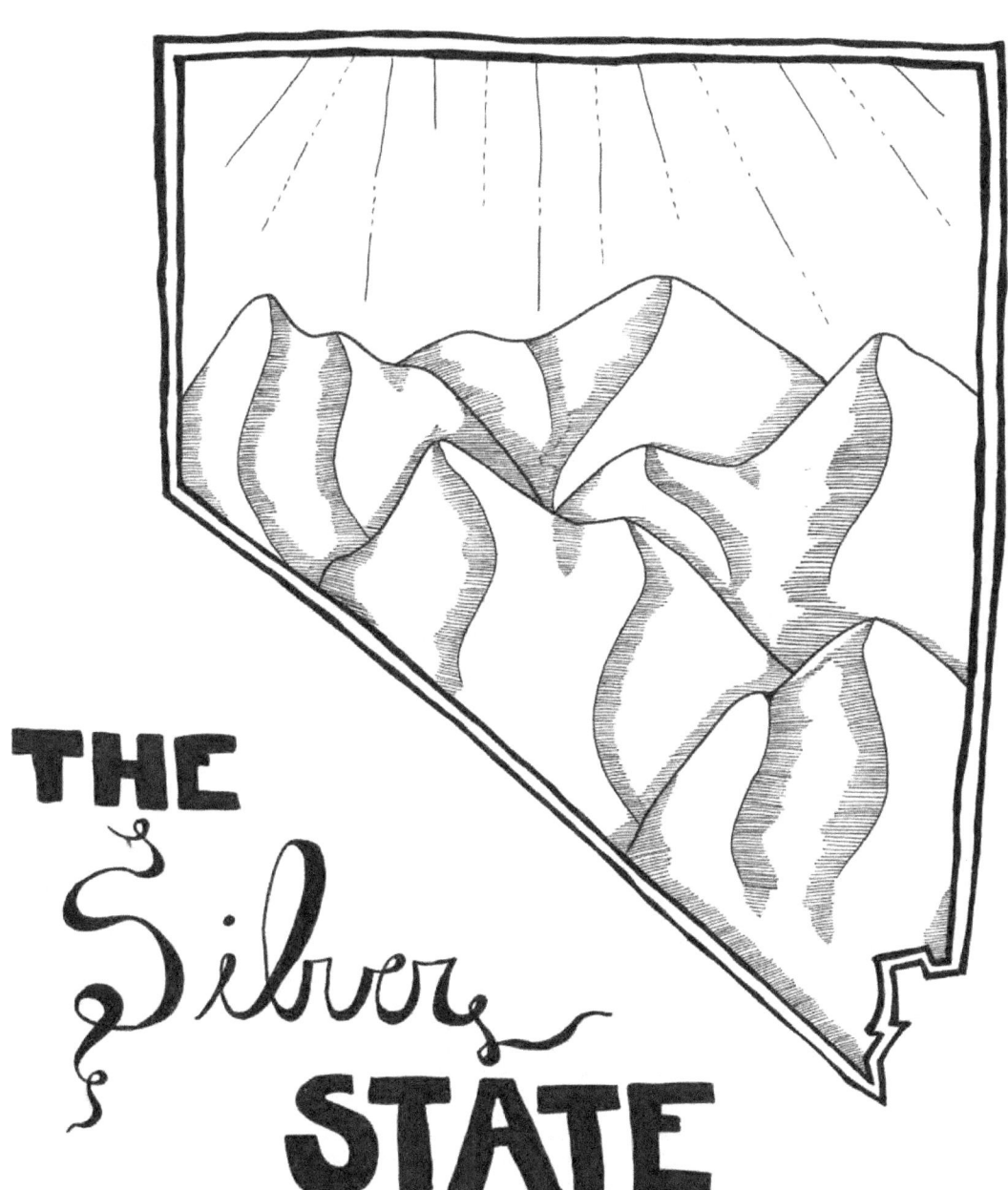

THE Silver STATE

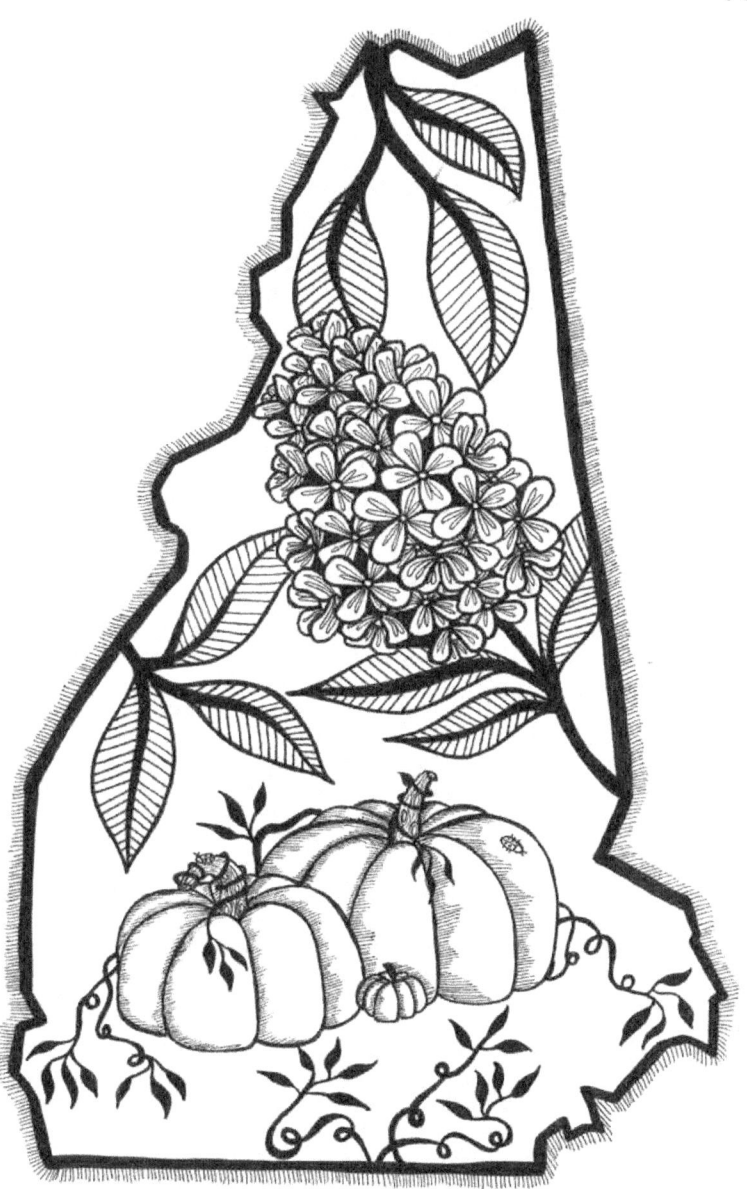

New Hampshire

The GRANITE STATE

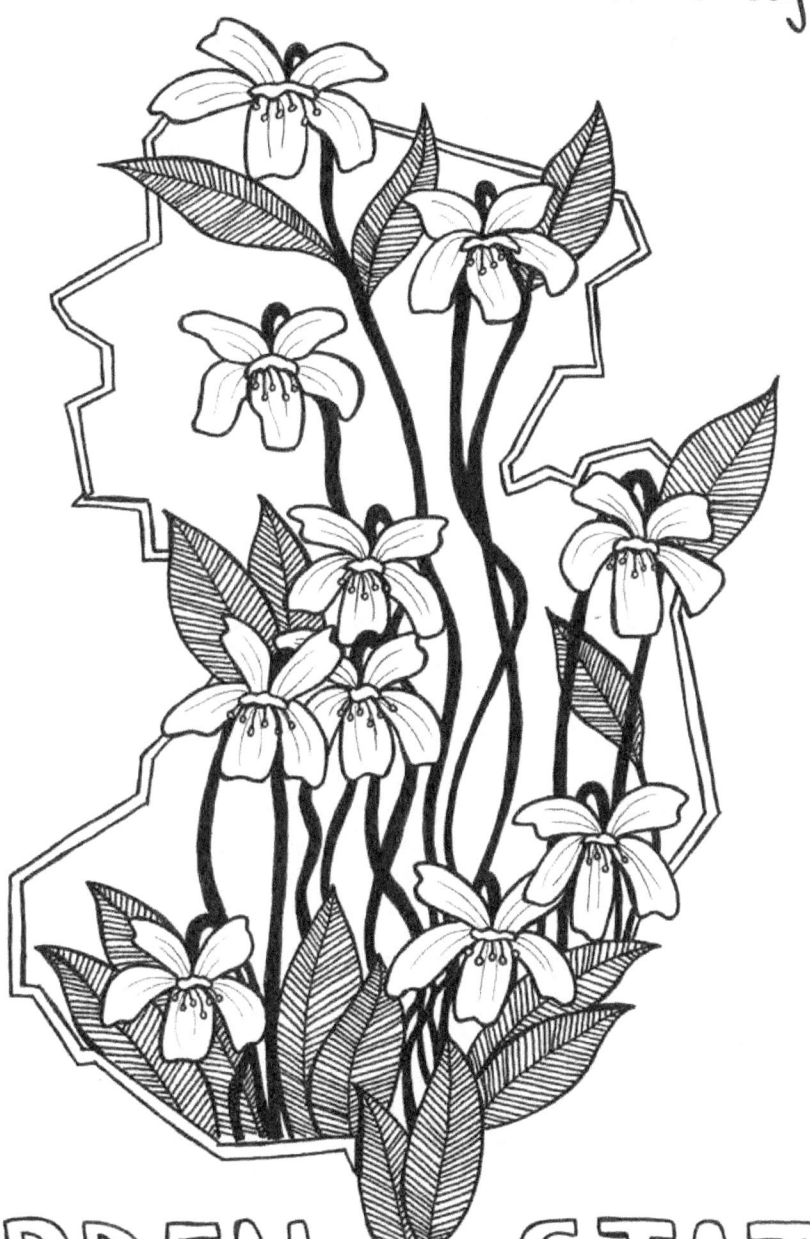

New Mexico

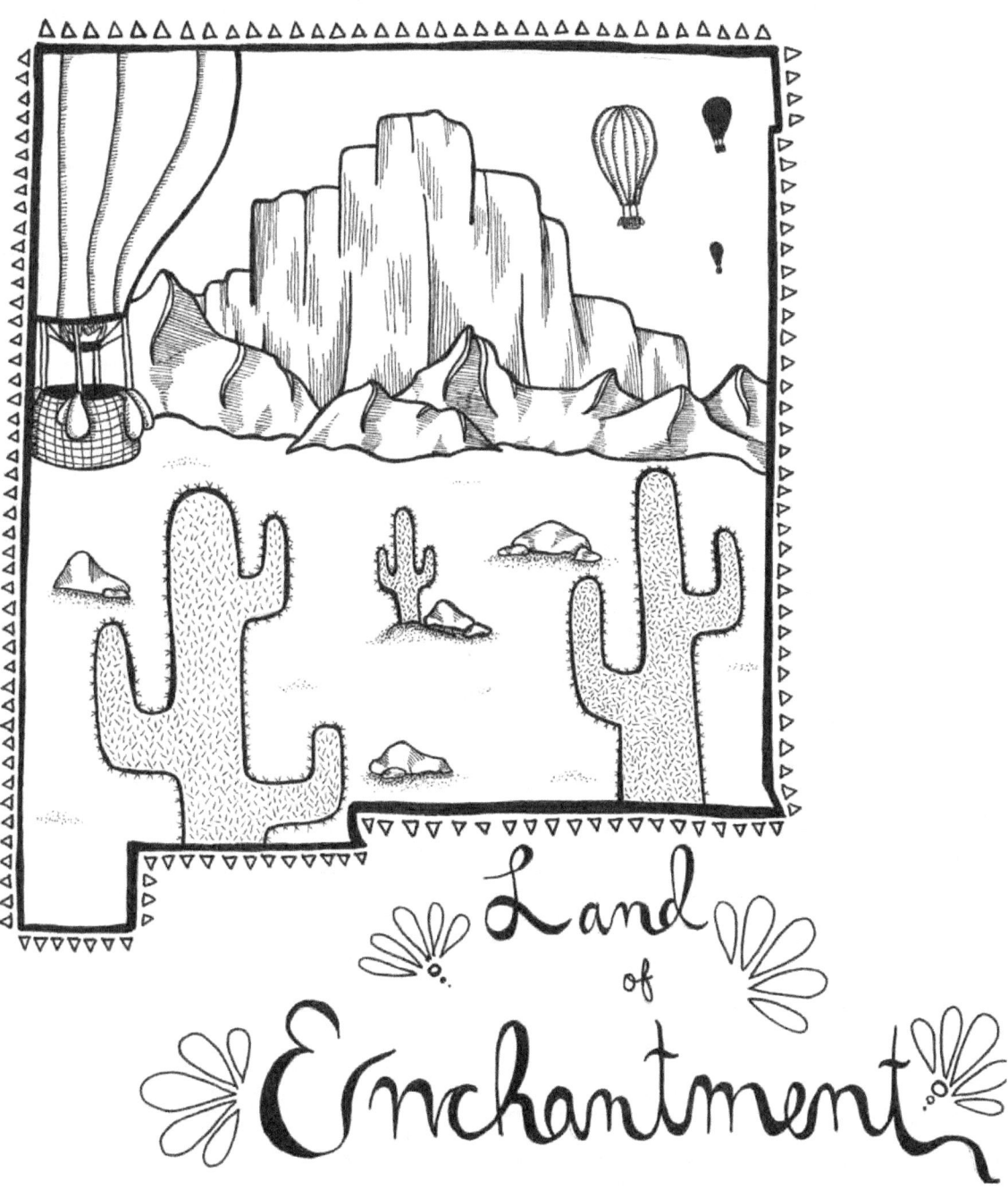

Land of Enchantment

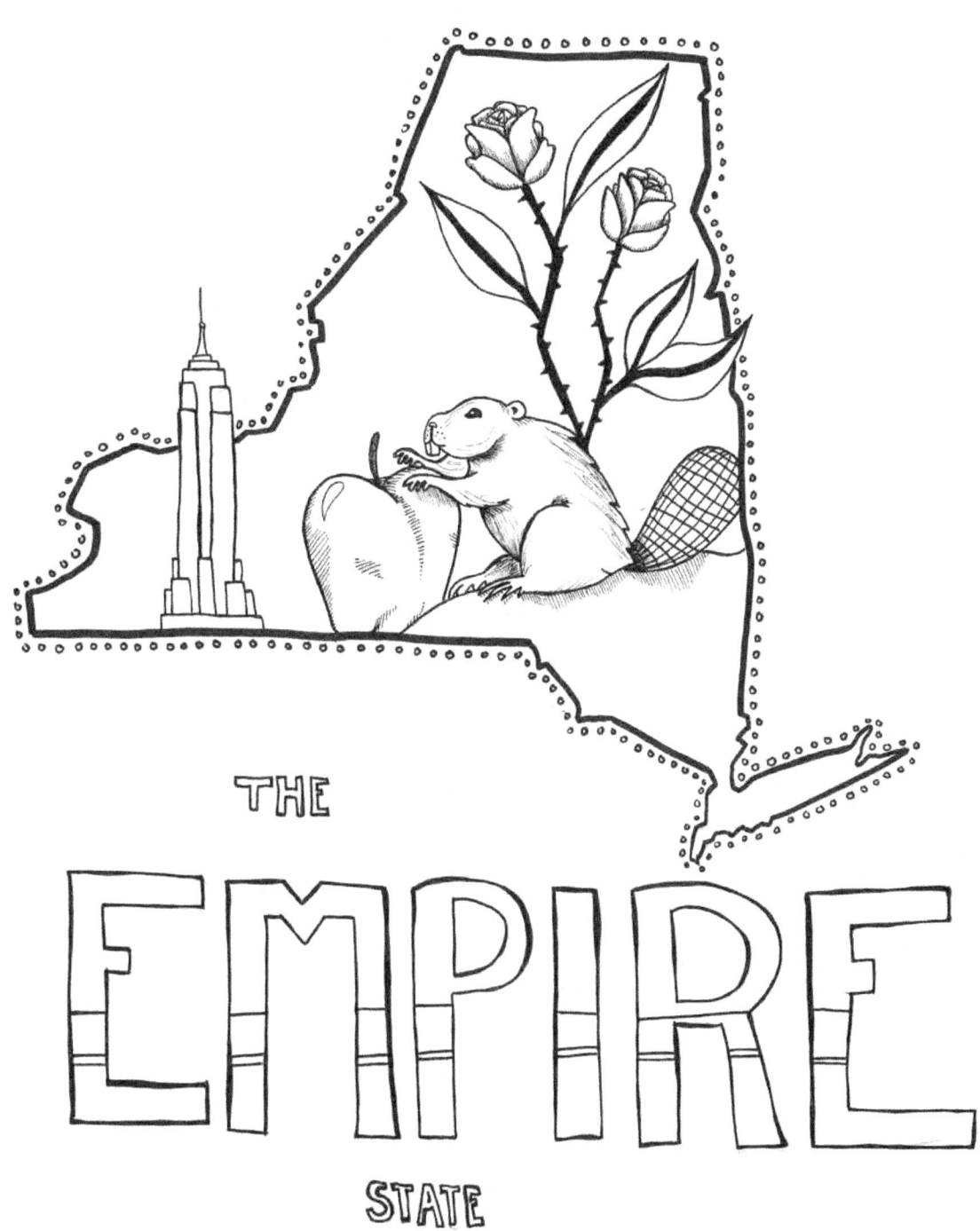

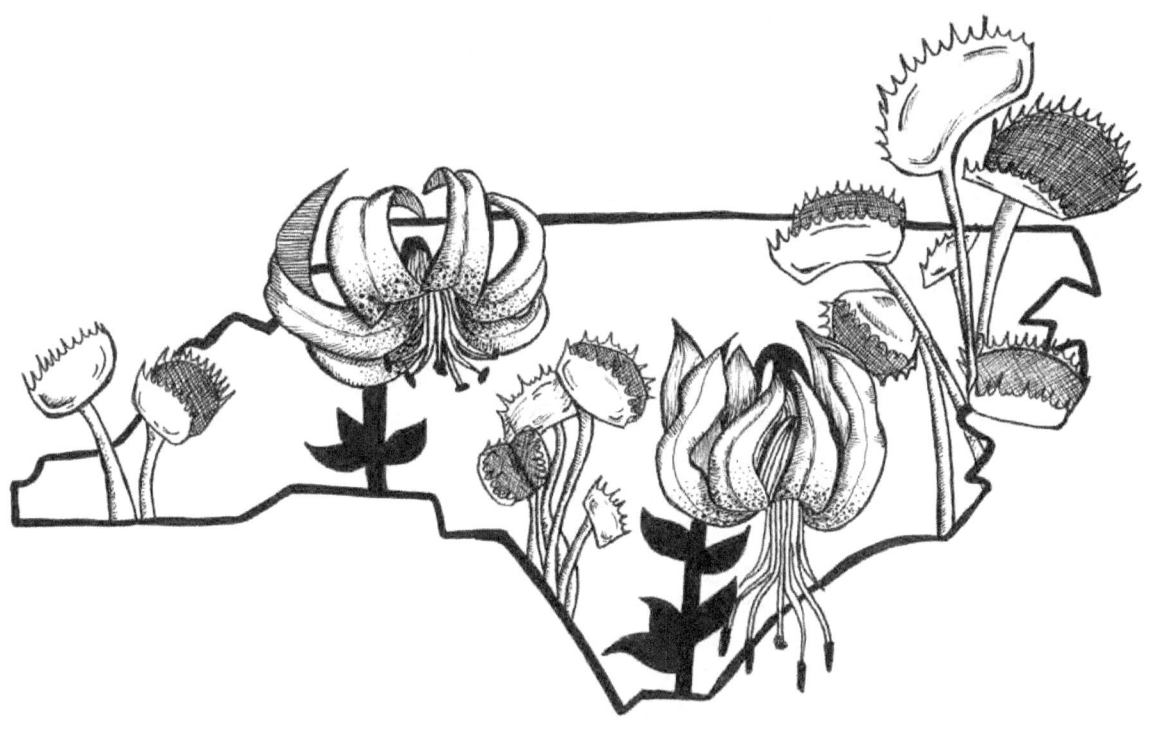
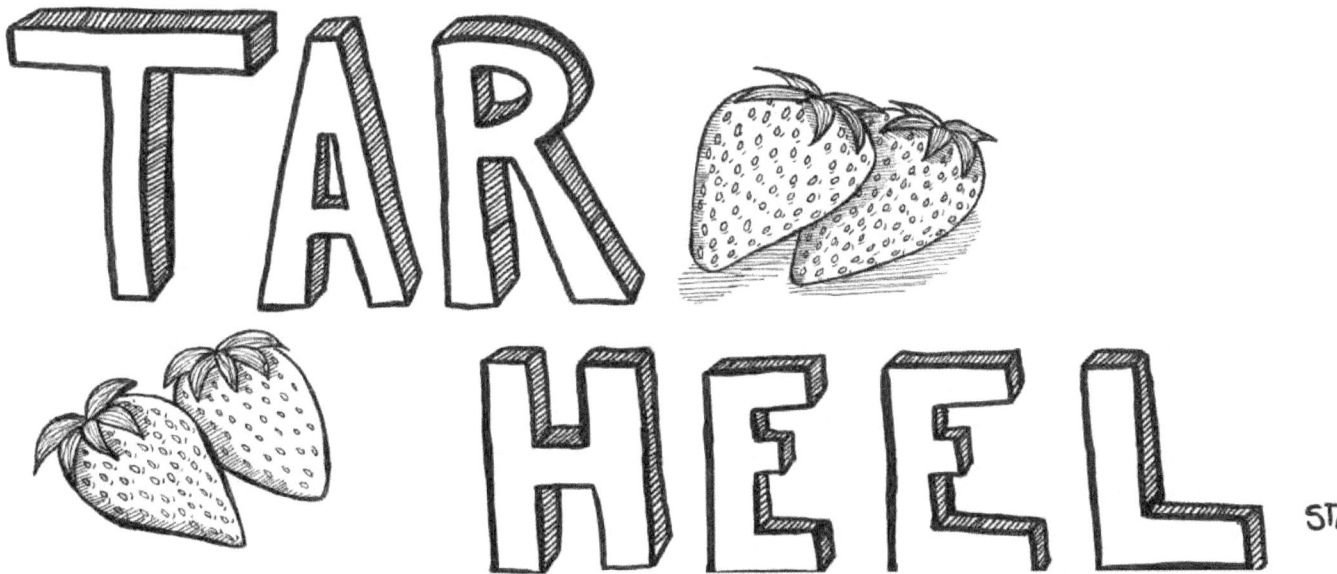

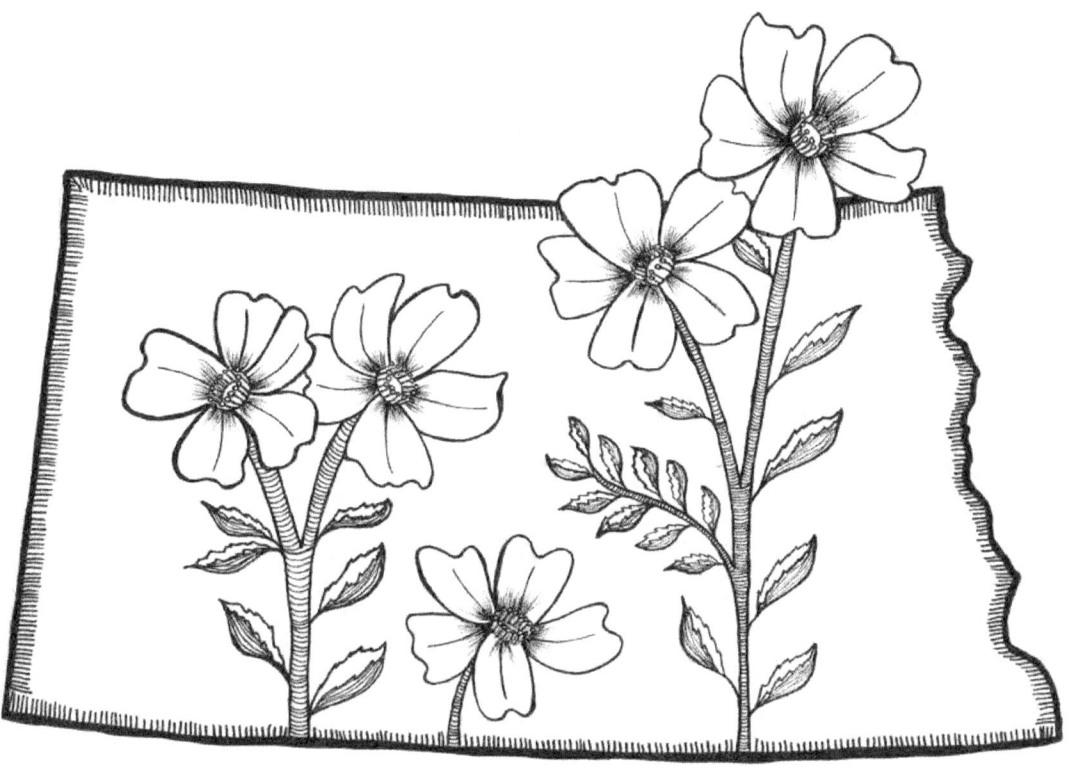

Ohio

THE Buckeye STATE

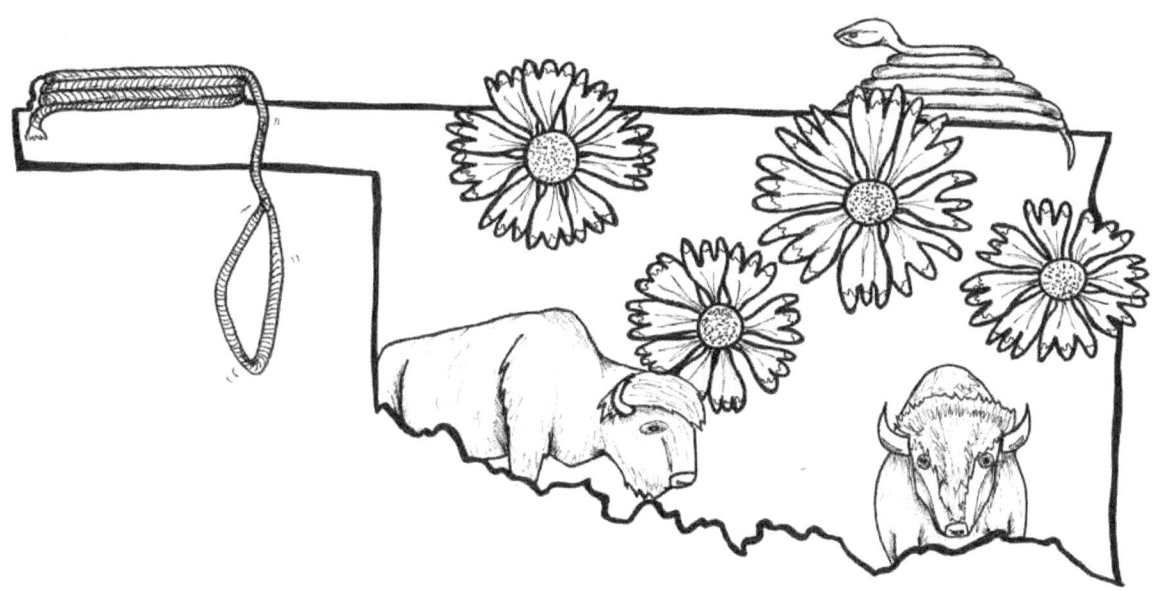

Oregon

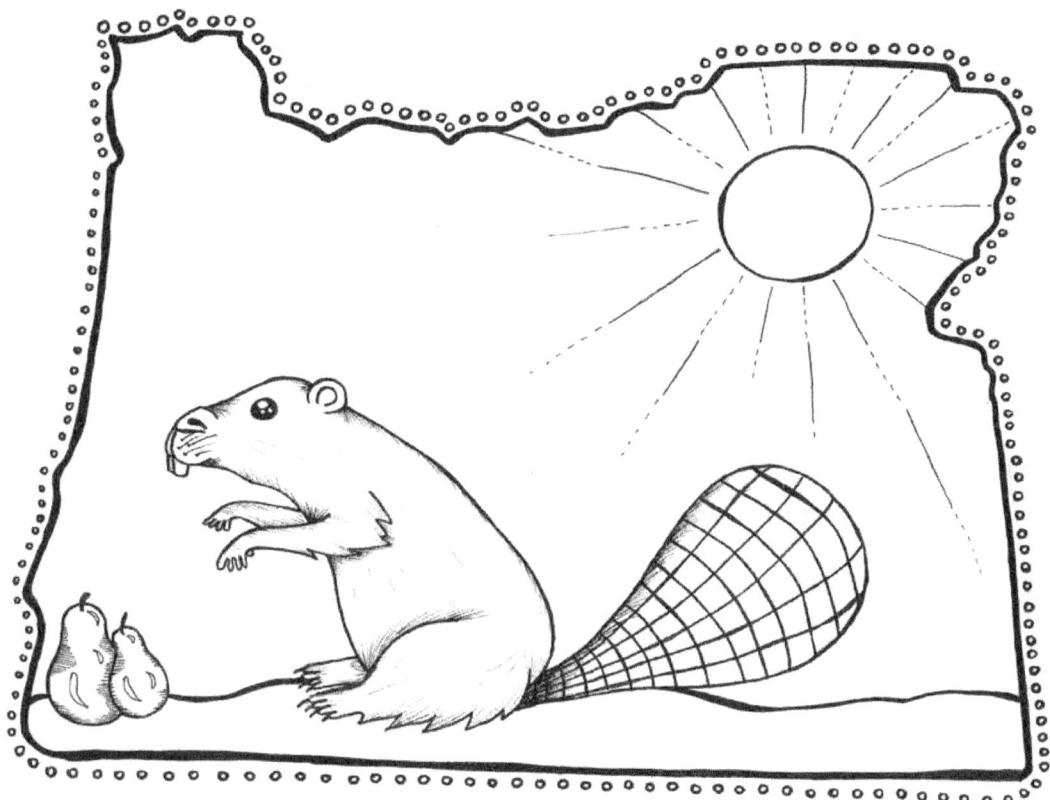

THE BEAVER STATE

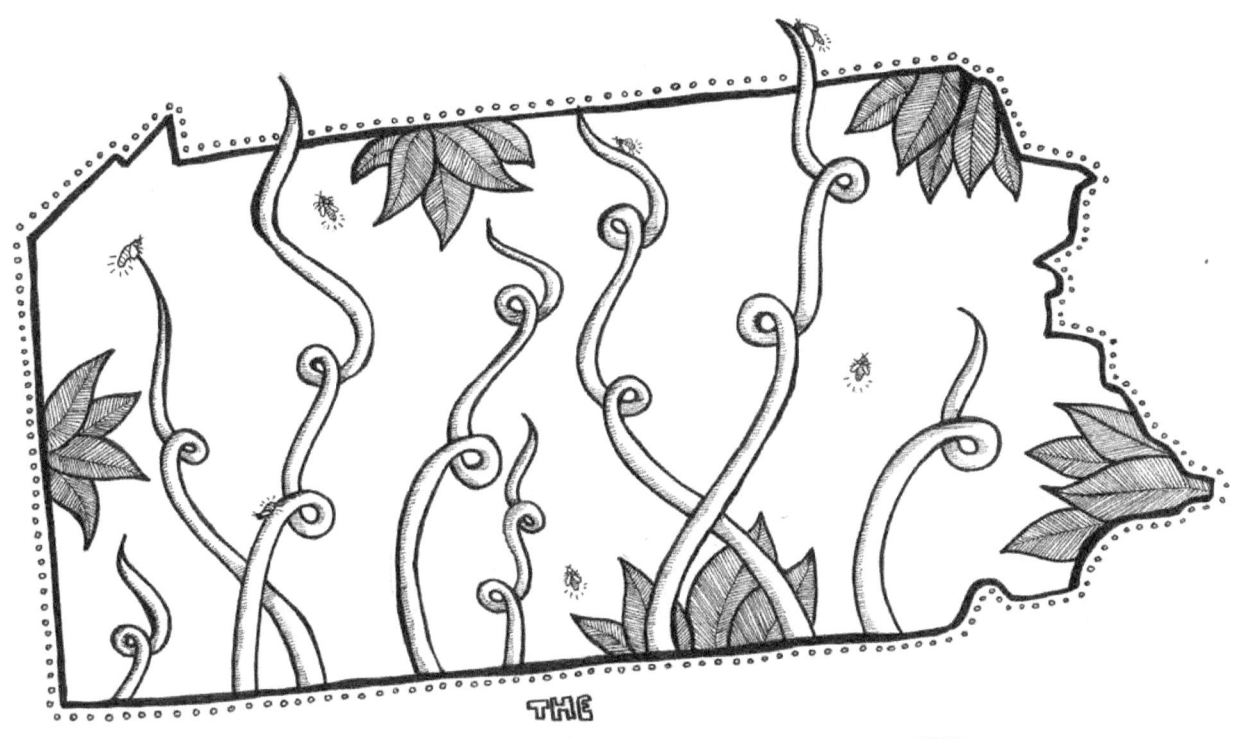

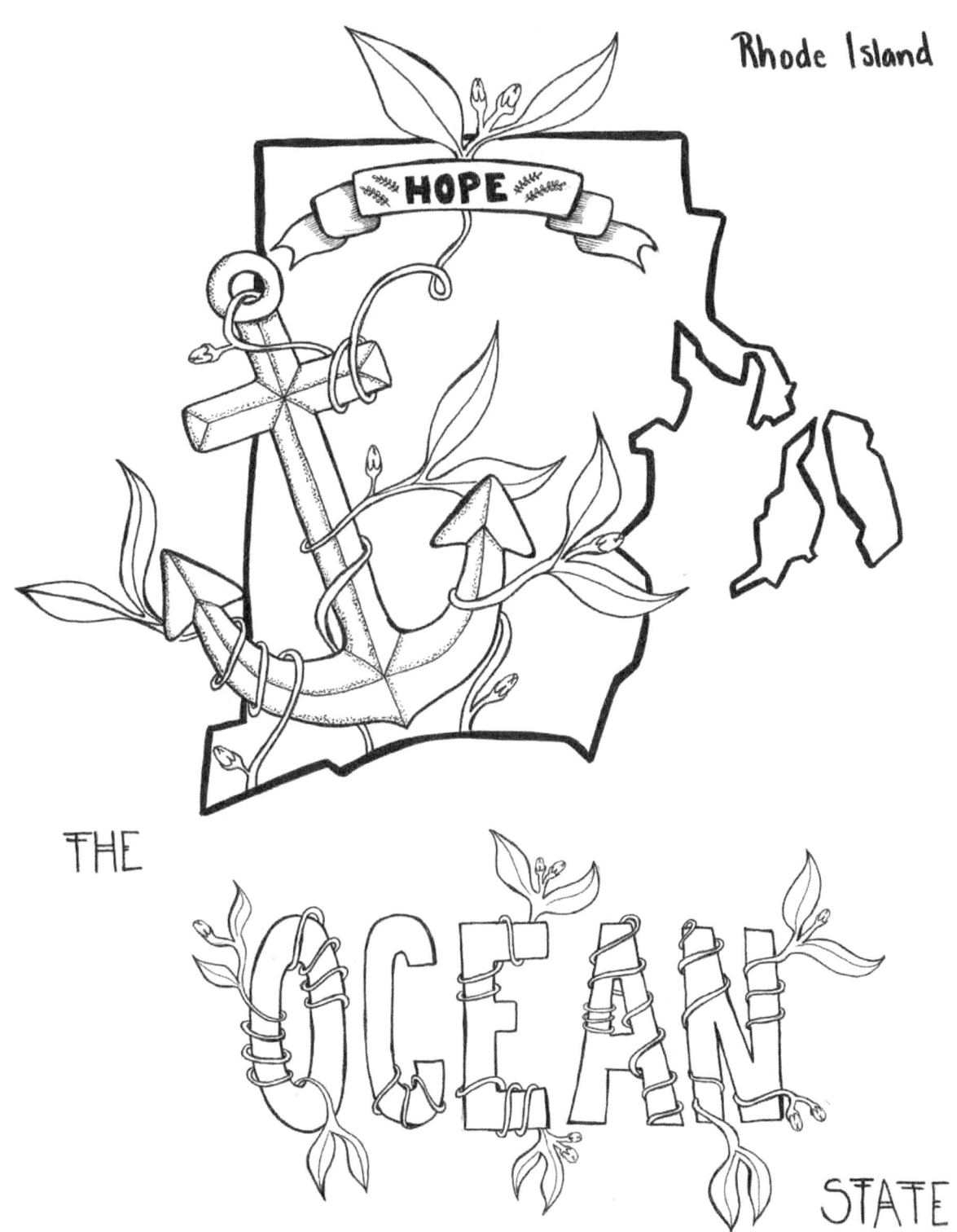

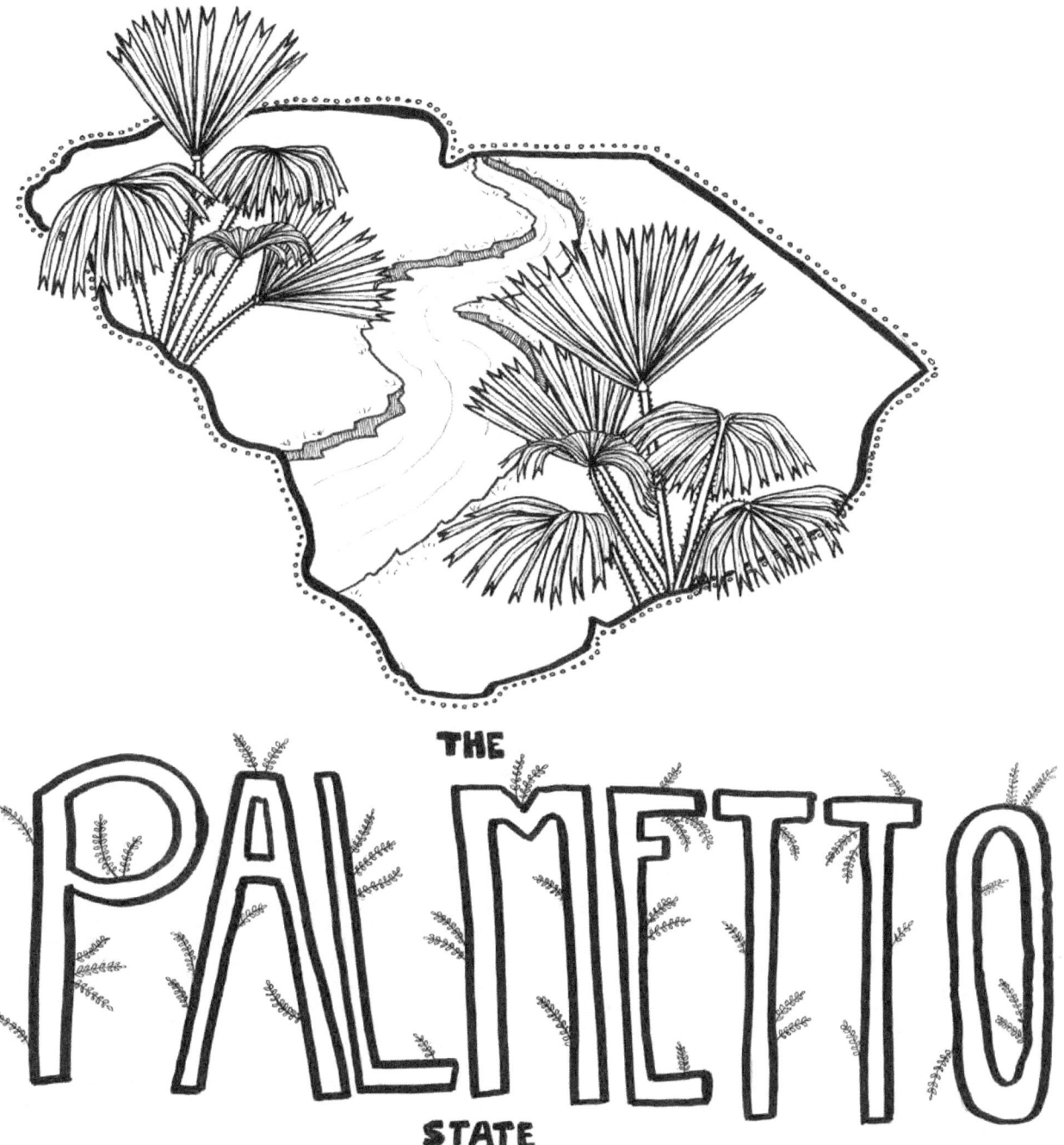

South Dakota

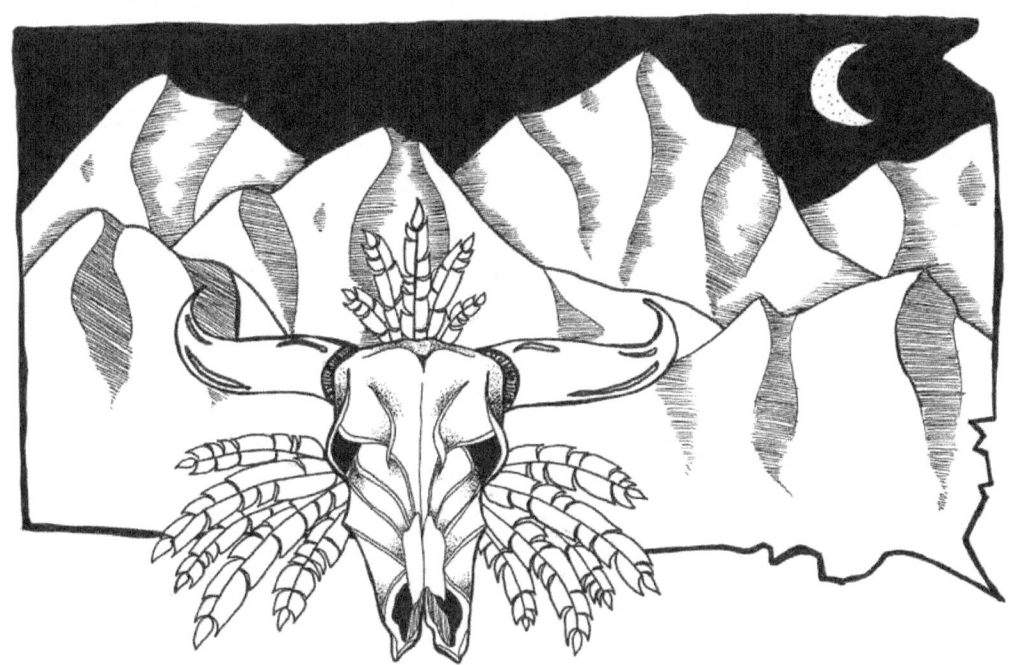

MOUNT Rushmore STATE.

Tennessee

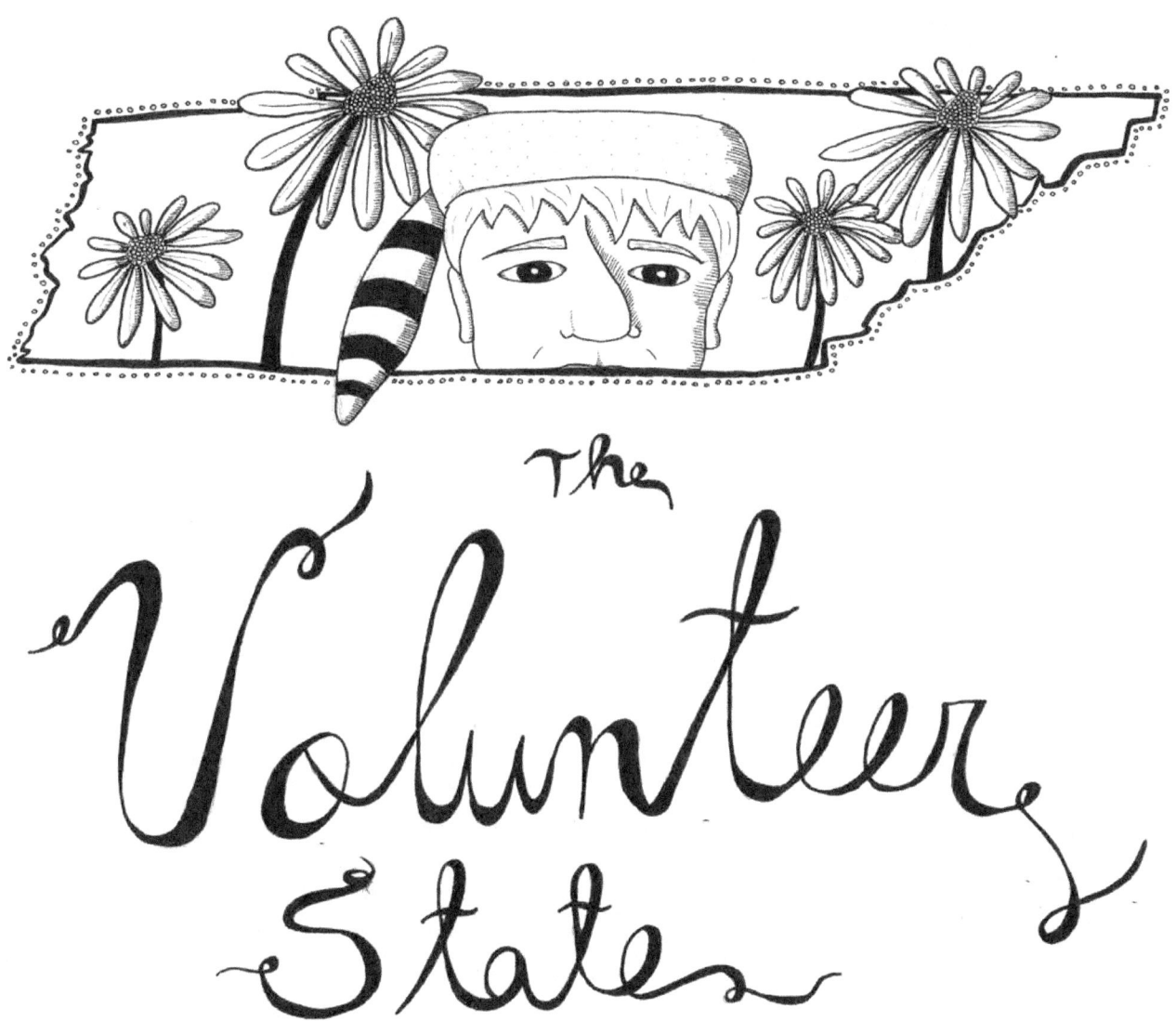

The Volunteer State

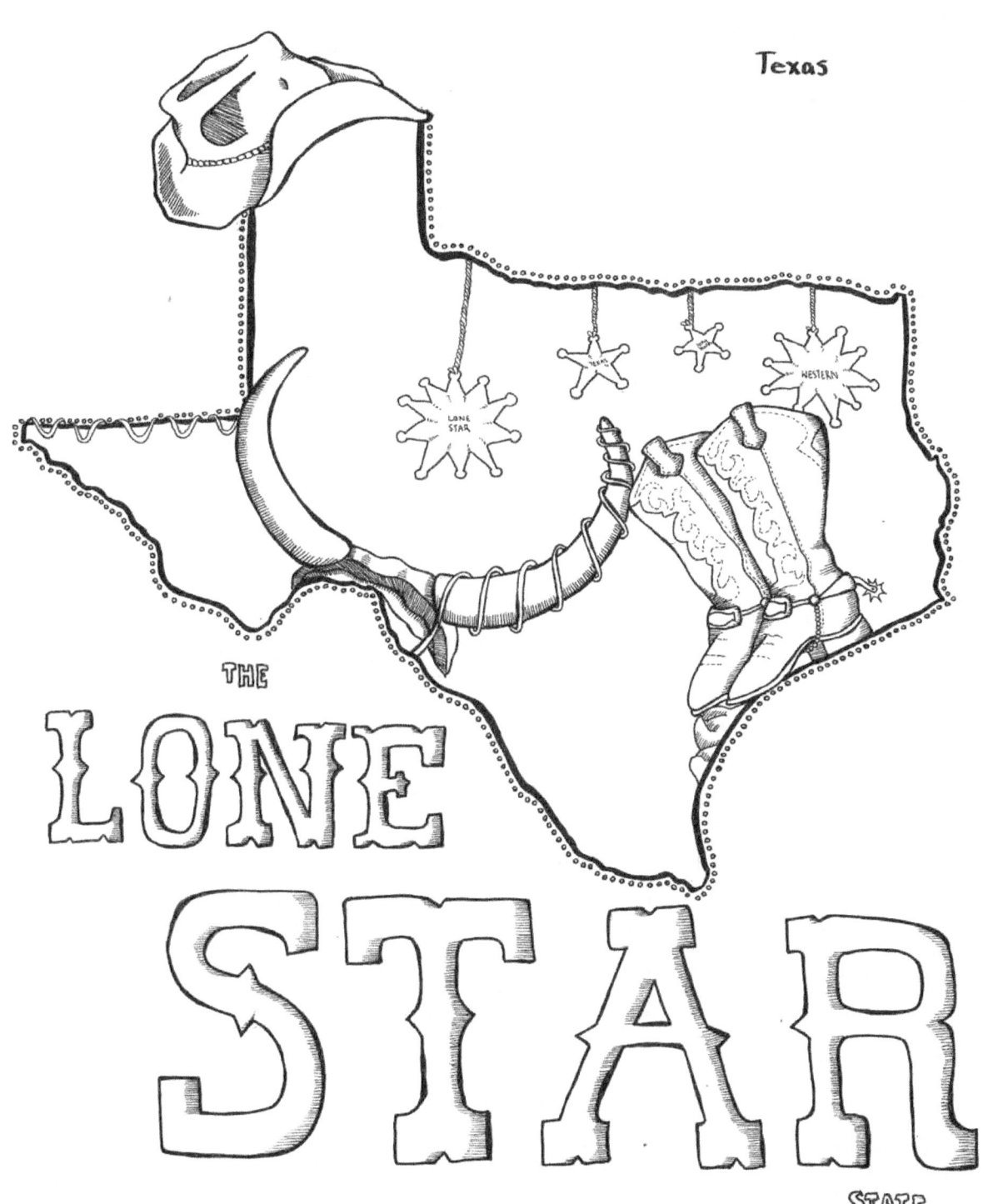

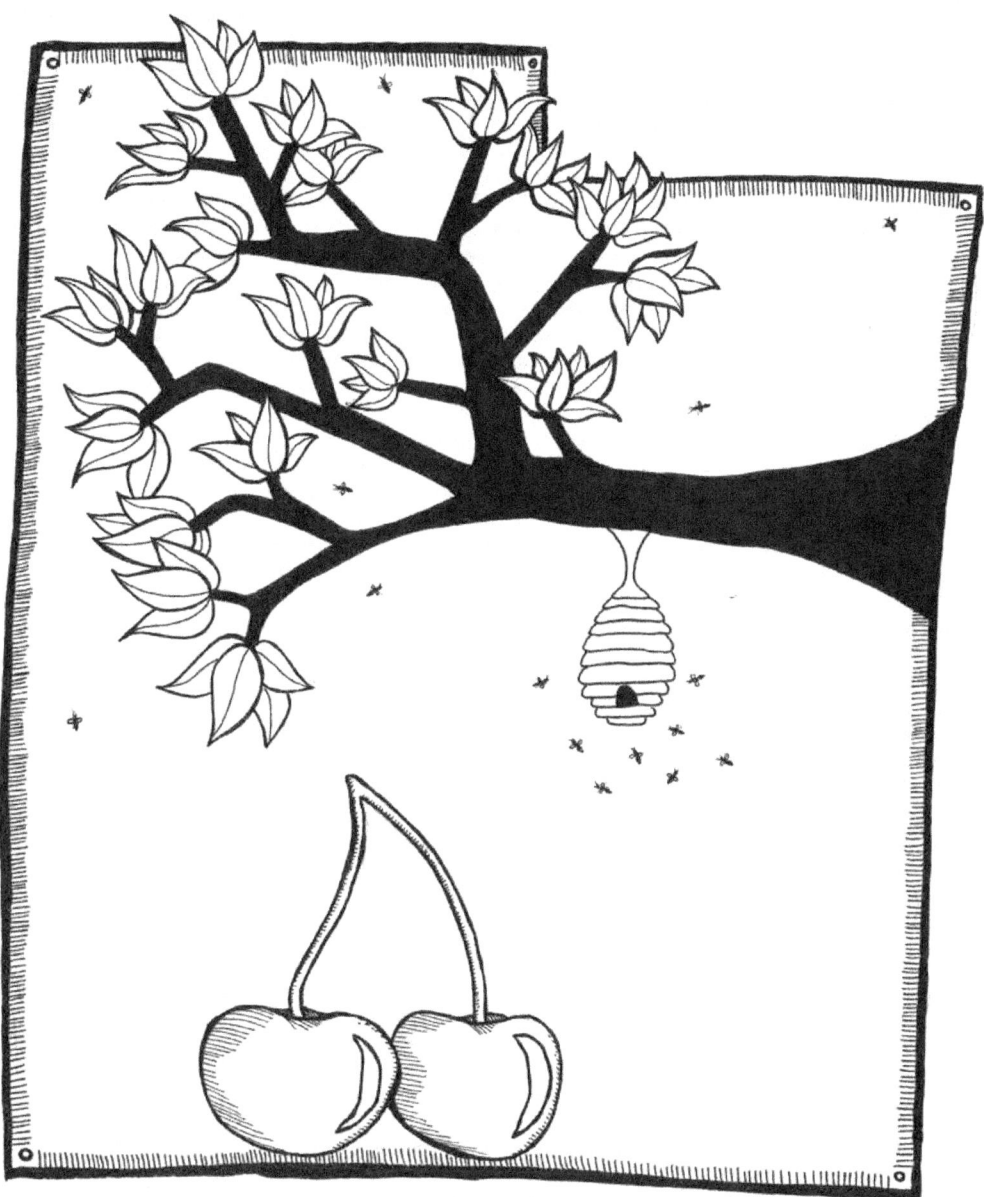

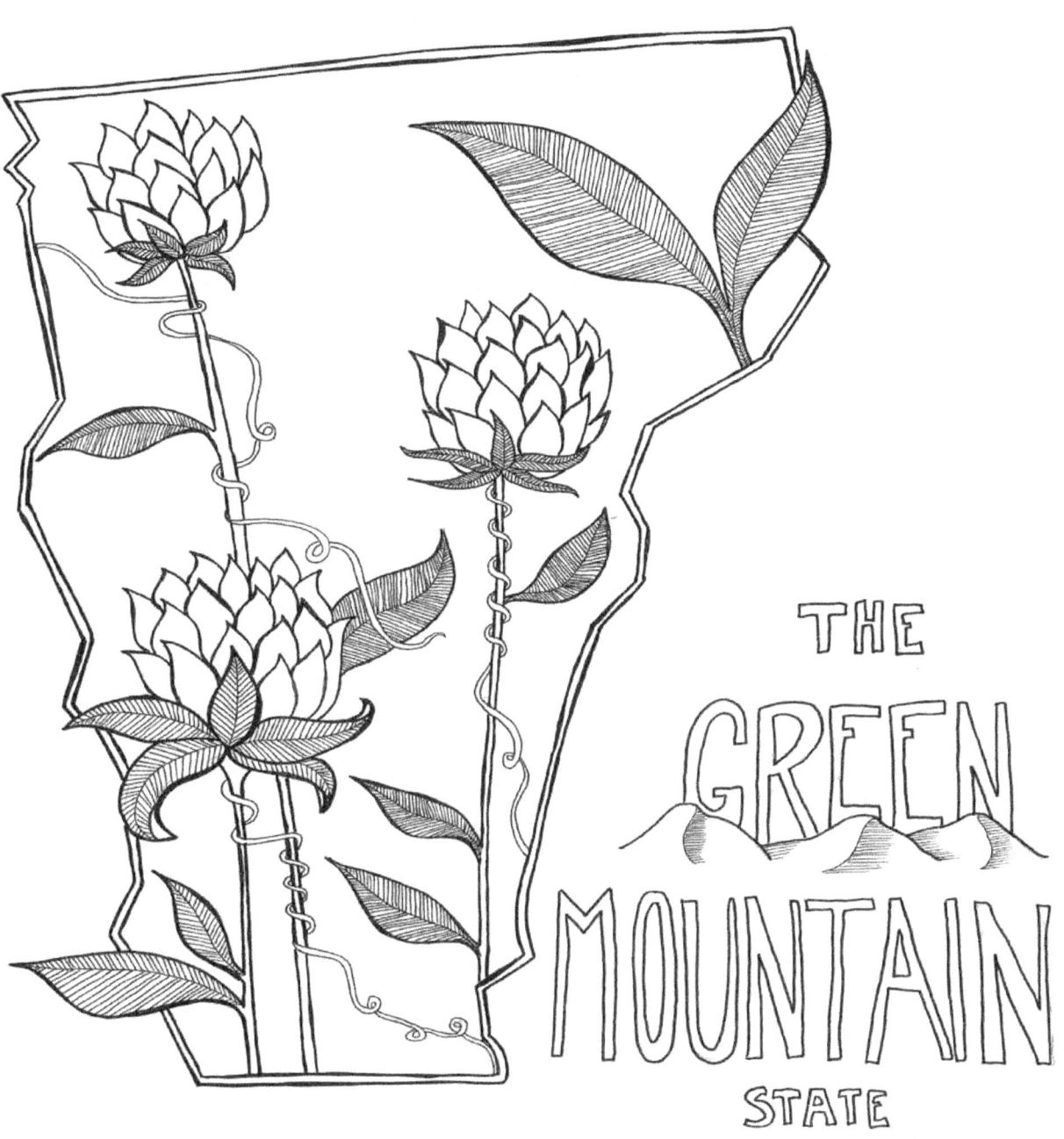

Virginia

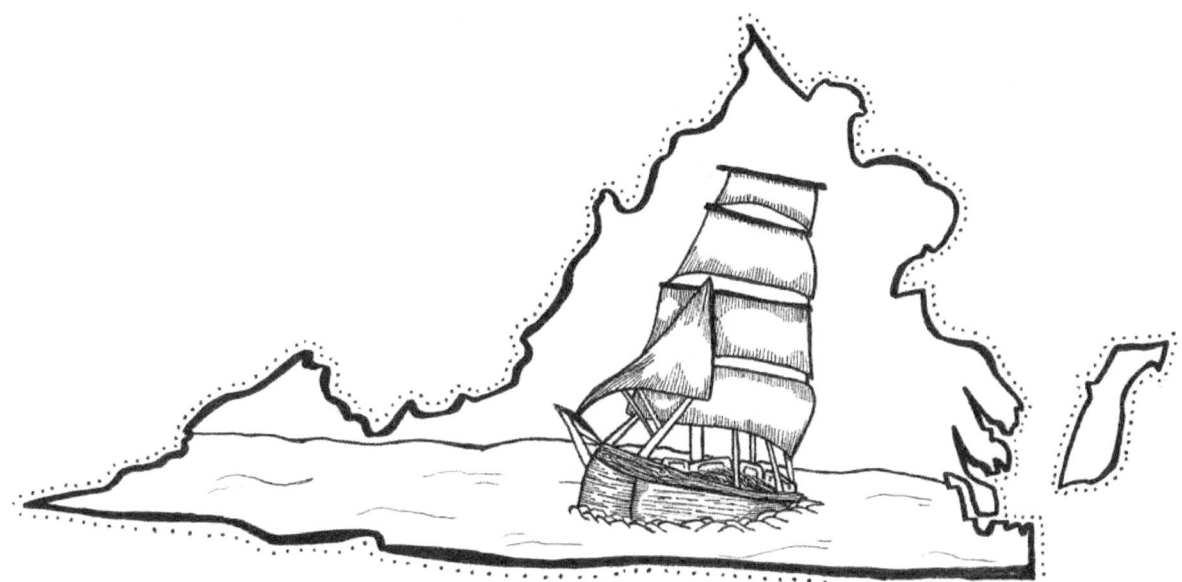

Old Dominion

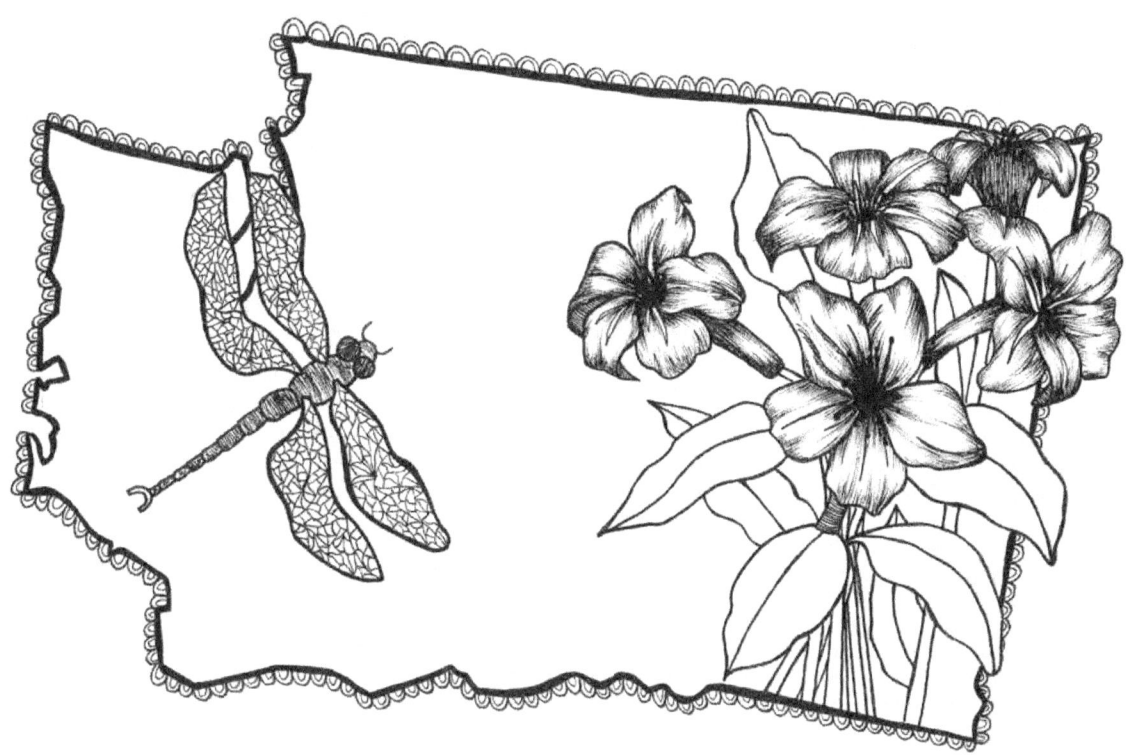

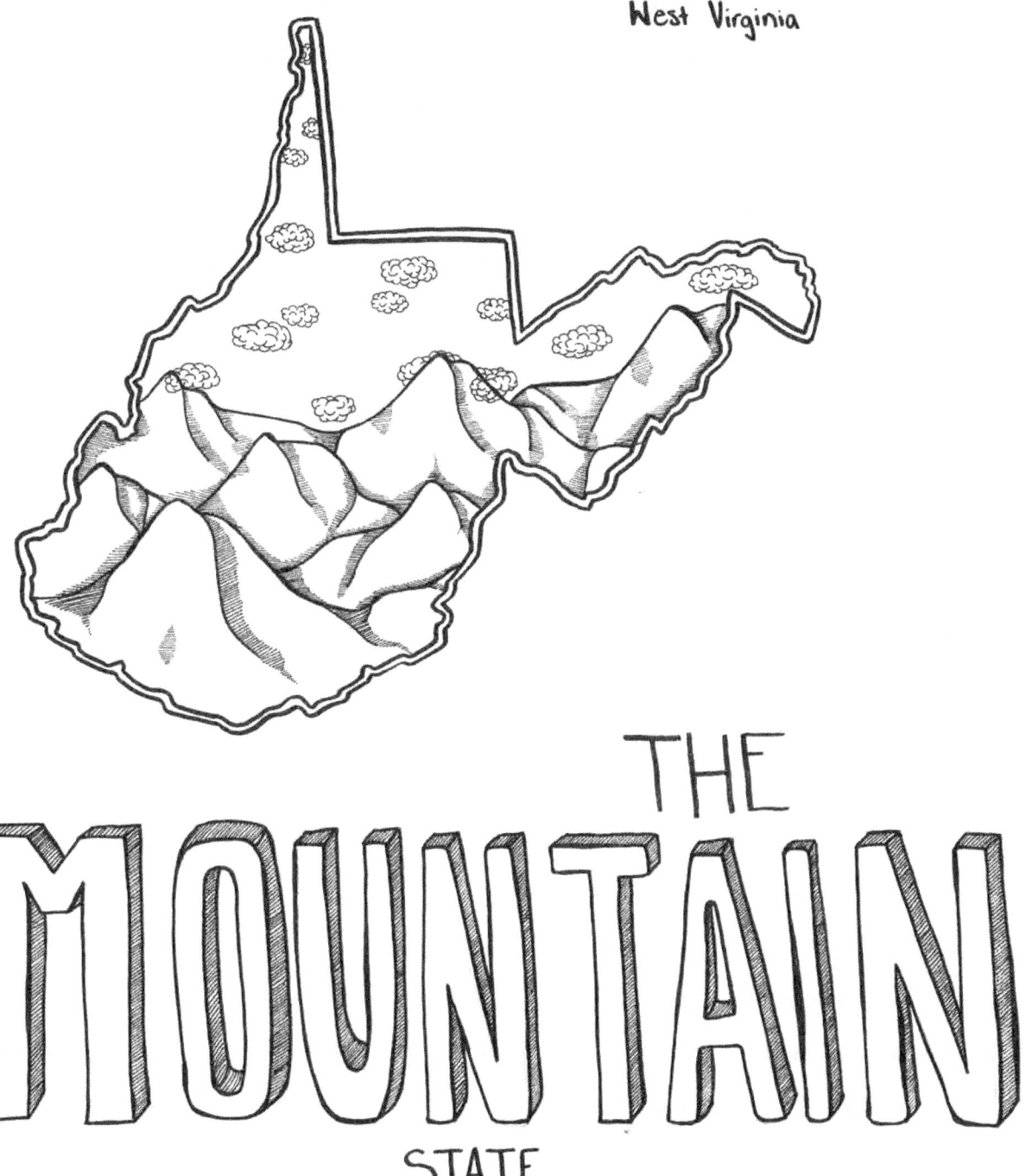

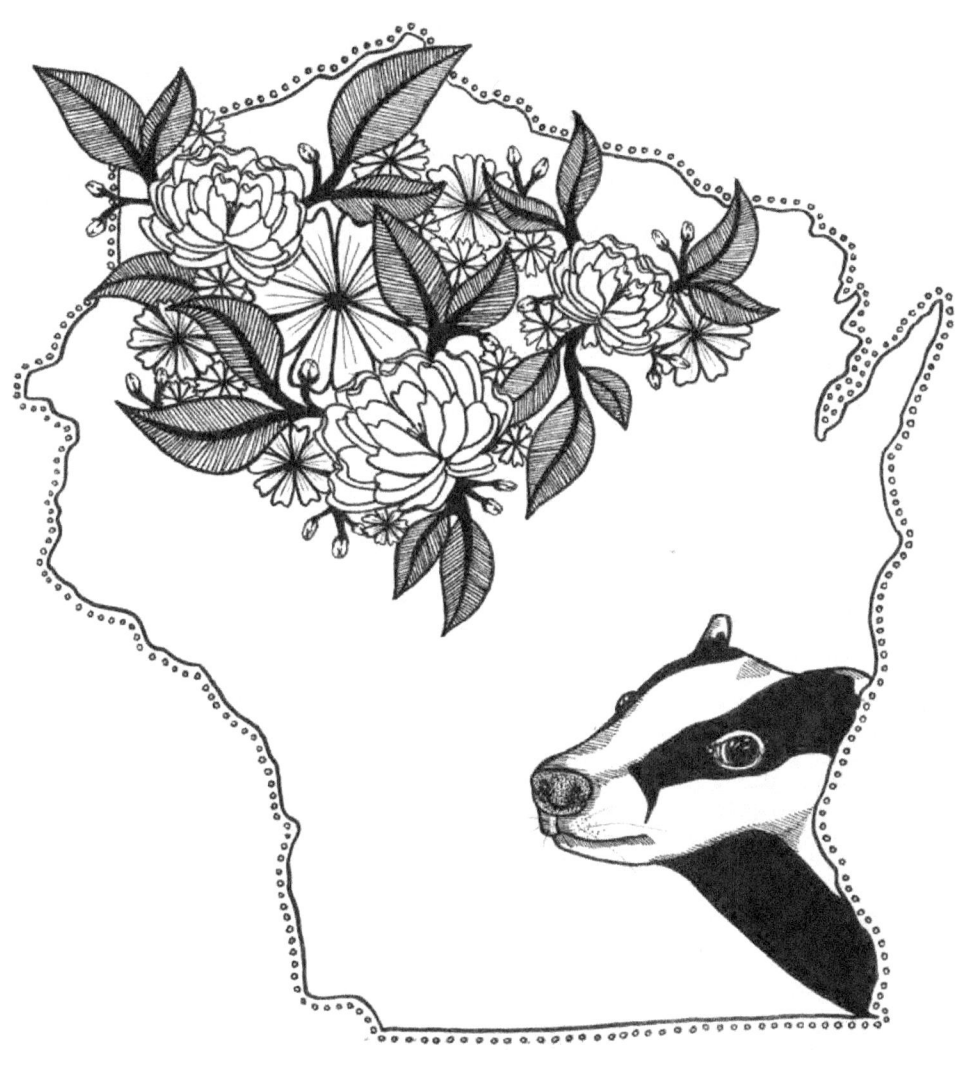
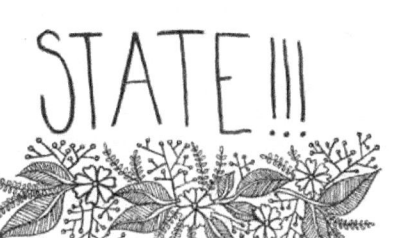

Wyoming

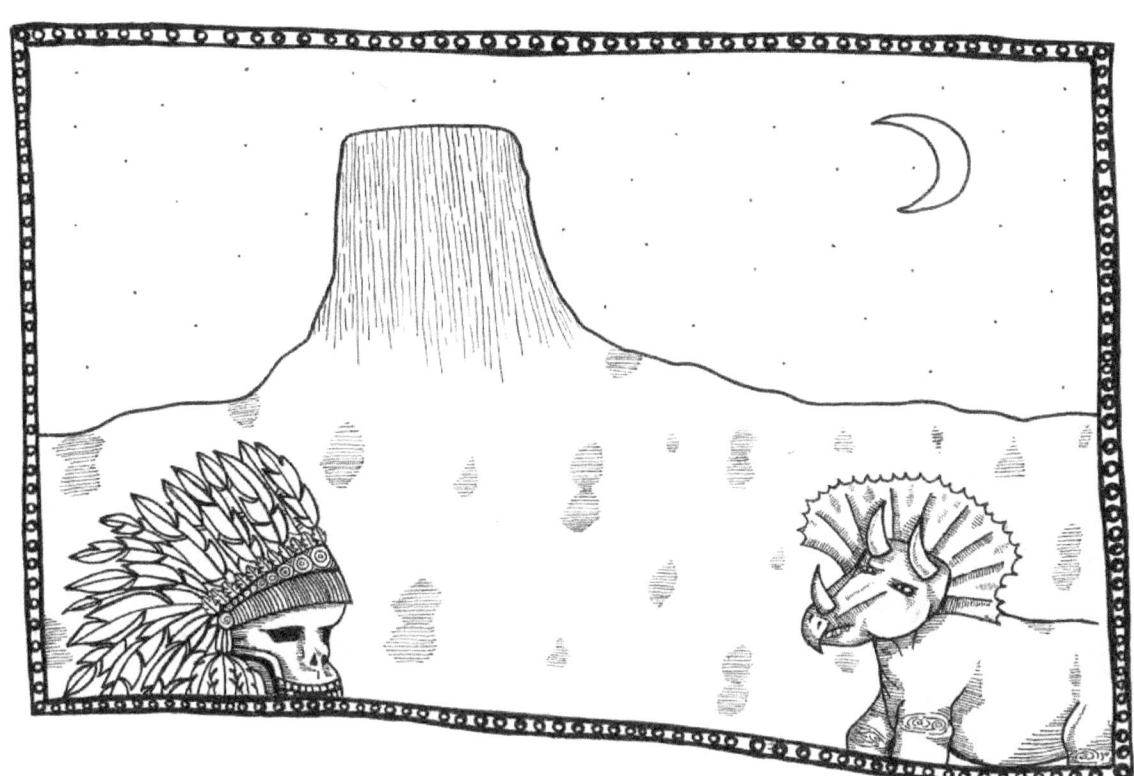

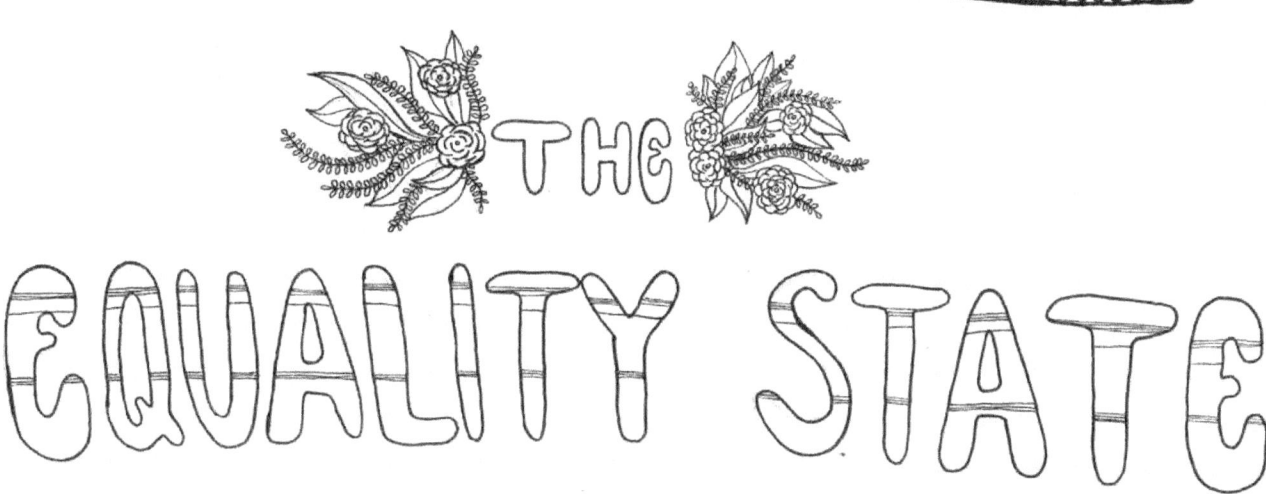

www.ingramcontent.com/pod-product-compliance
Lightning Source LLC
Chambersburg PA
CBHW062222220526
45471CB00009B/3311